Garden of Grief

Garden of Grief

Cultivating New Life After Loss

Lori Koidahl

Cover and interior design by Tabitha Lahr

Published 2020
Printed in the United States of America
Print ISBN: 978-1-7351156-0-3
E-ISBN: 978-1-7351156-1-0

Library of Congress Control Number: 2020911024

To my mom, Kathy.

Giver of life, love, and loss. You are the reason I love unconditionally; know the heartache of loss and the positive transformation it can bestow.

Your energy and spirit live on in me and your grandsons. We walk this earth because of you. I am forever grateful.

Love,
Your daughter, Loverdolly

Contents

A Mother's Message

Play, run
Engage in magical fun
Be present, be aware
Free yourself to go anywhere.

—Lori Koidahl

Vision

As I open an email on my phone and struggle to read
the increasingly small type
I am reminded of you
The woman who gave birth to me and raised me on
her own

I watched you struggle to read menus, pulling them
at arm's length
Hoping that would make things a bit more clear

It made me chuckle how cute you were doing this act
You'd give in and put your reading glasses on

A colorful pair
Pushed down at the end of your nose
A memory I cherish today
A simple act I never thought would mean anything

As I age and have more in common with you
These threads of familiarity weave into my life

Like bonds of love we can no longer form together

Author's Note

To write this book, I relied upon my personal journals I wrote during a three year period, which began when my mom died. I also used emails, scrapbooks, photo albums, videos, voice recordings, newspaper articles, legal documents, and police reports to recall events and research facts. I consulted with several people who appear in the book and called upon my own memory of this time in my life.

Grief defined by *Psychology Today:*

> Grief is the acute pain that accompanies loss. It
> is deep, because it is a reflection of what we love,
> and it can feel all-encompassing. Grief can follow
> the loss of a loved one, but it is not limited to
> people; it can follow the loss of a treasured animal
> companion, the loss of a job or other important
> roles in life, the loss of a home or of other posses-
> sions of significant emotional investment. It often
> occurs after a divorce.
>
> Grief is complex; it obeys no formula and has
> no set expiration date. It is an important area of
> ongoing research. While some experts have pro-
> posed that there are stages of grief—denial, anger,
> bargaining, depression, acceptance—others
> emphasize that grief is a very individualized emo-
> tion and not everyone grieves the same way.

Grief is sometimes compounded by feelings of guilt and confusion over a loss, especially if the relationship was difficult. Some individuals experience prolonged grief, sometimes called complicated grief, which can last months or years. Without help and support, such grief can lead to isolation and chronic loneliness. Many of the symptoms of grief overlap with those of depression. There is sadness, often loss of the capacity for pleasure; insomnia; and loss of interest in eating or taking care of oneself. But the symptoms of grief tend to lessen over time, although they may be temporarily reactivated by important anniversaries or thoughts of the loss at any time. And unlike depression, grief does not usually impair a sense of self-worth.

My soul-crushing grief occurred on June 19, 2007. My mom, a pedestrian crossing the street, was hit by a truck and killed when a young man ran a red light. Six other people were injured, but she was the only one who died. She was fifty-six years old. I was thirty-seven and my two boys, her tenderhearted grandsons, were eleven and six. I was not ready for her to go. She was such a young and vibrant woman full of life with ample years to live. Selfishly I still needed my mom, my best friend. I was furious that she'd died in a car crash, just like my dad and Uncle Rick, her brother, before her. It was hard to believe that so many important people in my family had all been killed in car crashes. It made me question how life could be so cruel and I wondered, *why me?*

Grief is a profoundly personal journey and can only be navigated in the way that works for the individual. It can take you to your deepest depth of sadness and crack your shell of self-protection. In my case, I can look back at grief as a catalyst for my rebirth and navigating the world in a new way. What I learned through this experience and how it changed my life informs this book. When you tell your story, you free yourself and give others permission to acknowledge their own story. I share my journey here as others did with me. Other people helped me feel not so alone, to be connected, and I could see myself in them. I saw how grief could be something to offer change in oneself and I learned to be open to what the universe had to offer. You never know what transformation is waiting for you right around the corner. I hope my story can do the same for you. Offer you some peace, connectedness, and a new way to look at grief.

CHAPTER 1:

Just Do It!

"What hurts us is what heals us."
—Paulo Coelho

There's no handbook on how to grieve, and the last thing I wanted was someone telling me that "time heals all wounds" and "this too shall pass." It has been many years now since my mom died. I can hear these kinds of platitudes now and not get pissed off. I can actually agree with them to some extent. But when you are so raw from your grief, the last thing you want to hear is that time will heal you. Because time means later down the road; and you hurt like hell right now. Time also meant more years without my mom, and I didn't want to think that there might come a point in the future when I wouldn't be sad about losing her. Would I ever be healed? If I wasn't sad, was that disrespecting her and her memory? Our time together? At the time I felt this to be true. I can see now it wasn't time that healed me, but the actions I took to heal. If I hadn't chosen to do certain things, there would have been no amount of time that would have healed my wounds. Honoring my grief journey gave me the peace and transformation I couldn't have imagined and didn't know I needed.

I read somewhere that grief is like a propellant to the fire already inside of you. If this is true, then I was not being my true self before she died. My mom's death brought who I was to the surface. My soul bubbled up. It's like I came back to myself, to the essence of who I always was. All of us have access to this as children, when we have no inhibitions, no goals to attain, no ill will toward others. Along the way, we start to feel the pressures of society and we start to "should" ourselves. I should do this, I should do that. I should be a certain way to be accepted and successful. It can turn your attention outside of yourself to attaining instead of being who you truly are. What we're left with is a stunning soul—longing to be ourselves and to connect deeply with others.

I embarked on a Hero's Journey when my mom died. When you travel on this kind of pilgrimage, you are forever changed. There is no going back. You have a new fervor for life. I was the protagonist in this story, navigating through the deep sorrow of loss and traversing a whole slew of emotions. I was transformed by my grief adventure. I gained wisdom and new knowledge that I brought to my new world. This included slowing down, connecting with others, being relational, letting go, just being, doing what made me content, honoring my journey, and trusting my gut (my intuition) because my body felt it first.

In the words of Nike, "Just Do It!" There is no other way. The only way to heal is to go through your grief. You must feel it to heal it. It is yours and you will do it your way, because you are unique. Honor your journey and let it take you places you didn't know you needed to go. There is no right or wrong way to do it. It is personal to you and your relationship with the world.

Get angry
Be sad
Cry
Laugh
Take your time
Rest
Try new things
Be open
Follow your heart
Share your story
Connect
Read
Write
Create
Listen
Move your body
Dance
Pay attention
Be alone
Relate
Remember
Cherish the small stuff
Renew

CHAPTER 2:

Loverdolly

"Names are the sweetest and the most
important sound in any language."
—Dale Carnegie

What is in a name? We all come into this world named by
someone else. Some people choose to change their name as they
think the one given to them doesn't fit. Then there are celeb-
rities who change their names to something strikingly stage
worthy. I came into this world as Lori Jean Cook, a name that
had echoes of my father's name, Larry Gene Cook. A father I
never met. My parents were married only a month before he
fell asleep at the wheel and he died after being in a coma for
two months. My mom was only nineteen years old, my dad
sixteen. I loved my name because it made me feel like I was part
of this man my mother had loved, and she honored both of us
by making me his namesake.

My mom also dotingly called me Loverdolly, her term of endearment for me.

No one else has called me this and no one ever will. It is ours. I feel treasured when I think of her name for me. I was her only child and she my only parent. We had a close bond that grew stronger as I got older, especially once I had my own children. Raising children is no easy feat. It is a lifelong commitment with no instructions. Children are their own beings and come to this earth a little soul on their individual intimate adventure. You love them so deeply and want the best for them. You can nurture them, guide them, and walk through fire for them, but in the end, they make their own choices and decisions. You just want them to make the right ones to keep them safe and lead a life they enjoy.

I gained a new appreciation for my mom after having children. A number of the thoughts and stories I held onto that upset me about her I was able to let go of when I became a mom, and even more so after she died. What did it all matter now? I had held onto why she did this, why didn't she do that, why wasn't she different, but that was all wasted energy. There's no fixing another person. Ultimately, I arrived at the truth: she did the best she could, and she loved me. What else mattered? Knowing you're loved by someone is the gratification we all seek. I had that.

As a mother, I understood the unconditional love I had for my sons and could see and intuit that she carried that for me. I knew there was forever one person in the world who would love me no matter what. When my mom died, that person was gone. Who would care about me this deeply? I was alone in the world without her. I was an orphan. Other family members had died in my life, but none of that affected me so profoundly. I know the reason for this was our close mother-daughter relationship, and we were also best friends. Her death was a shock, and the circumstances were severely traumatic. Not expected at all. For me, this made a difference—the fact of her life being cut short and the feeling I carried that my time with her had been stolen.

When I was growing up, my mom would write me notes on little pieces of paper, addressing them to Loverdolly in her left-handed script. I loved her handwriting. It was kind of loopy, but perfectly legible. Unlike mine. My cursive is hard to read, even for me at times. For special occasions she'd put one of these notes in a card or a box. Like her own personally branded gift certificate just for me. "Loverdolly, Happy Valentine's Day! This is good for one pair of earrings. Love, Mom." I so wish I would have kept those notes. My loss feels compounded by no longer having them, or much else she had written to me over the years. I am more sentimental since her passing and now keep notes and cards from those dear to me. There's something so personal and touching when you have a letter, card, or note from someone you love, that's written by them, to you. It's a piece of them, an illustration of the relationship you shared, and a nugget of history to preserve the fact that they existed, and you were important to each other.

Here's an acrostic poem I wrote about my pet name, Loverdolly. It reminds me of something my mom would have given me.

L – Lori, loving, listener
O – open-minded, offering, observing
V – vulnerable, vital, valuable, validating
E – empathic, empowered, engaged, endearing, enlightened, embracing, expressing, energetic, emerging
R – Riley, reflecting, respecting, reminiscing
D – Dylan, delightful, dancing, determined, discovering, dreaming, dynamic, desiring
O – opportunistic, optimistic
L – laughter, letting go, longing
L – legacy, lessons, living
Y – yearning

I encourage you to save a couple notes, cards, or even the to-do lists of loved ones. Also be the giver, and write a little something to your loved ones that they can savor. These are tender treasures indeed.

CHAPTER 3:

Doing To Being

"Action is the antidote to despair."
—Clarissa Pinkola Estes

I learned at an early age that to get things done you have to act. Be in action. You can talk all you want, but action is the real deal. When my mom passed, it was no different. I got into action. It's my MO to do. Doing has consistently been what I've done best. I am a person who gets things done.

Let's back up a smidge to see how I got from being all-consumed by doing to getting to a more balanced place. In my adult years, I have gone to therapy, read self-help books, watched a treasure-trove of Oprah Winfrey (I love me some Oprah), listened to a plethora of podcasts, and taken part in the Landmark Forum's Curriculum for Living. Landmark is a personal and professional training and development program which opens your awareness to possibilities. All of this leads to who I am now—a more balanced and contemplative person. We all have a different path, and mine has been one of seeking and the desire to be more self-aware. It has been a bumpy and windy road at times, but it has been all mine. To become more self-aware, you must be open-minded and willing to see yourself in others: the good, the bad, and the ugly.

I am not saying doing is a bad thing. In fact, the quote at the beginning of the chapter—"Action is the antidote to despair"—illustrates the opposite. Action can be the answer, but it can also consume you and run you ragged. There is a state called being. And we are human *beings*. Not human *doings*. We need to just "be" sometimes. In this space there is room for quiet and self-reflection. Stop the doing, the noise, the action, the addiction to getting things done. I wasn't *being* before my mom died. I was *doing*. Doing a deluge of dutiful deeds. Her death brought me to the realization that I needed more balance in my life.

Growing up with a single mom, I saw how hard it was for her to get a good-paying job with the little education she'd completed. I vowed I'd get a college degree and a high-paying job. From a young age I was independent and goal-oriented. My mom was surprised and particularly proud when I told her I was going to a four-year university. I saw that action would help me fulfill my goals. I lived at home and worked during college to optimize my money and time. I was not your typical college student. I didn't have the carefree college experience because I was focused more on accomplishing my goals. I was married one year after college at twenty-three, bought my first house at twenty-four, and had my first child, Riley Roo, at twenty-five. Wow! I'm exhausted just writing about it.

I climbed the career ladder and by the time I was twenty-eight, my husband and I had bought our second home. I had my second child, Dilly Bear, at age thirty-one. I was busy doing—taking care of family, taking care of work, and neglecting to take care of myself. I was constantly "on" from when I woke up until I went to bed. Unfortunately, I had insomnia because I couldn't turn my brain off. I was so worried I'd miss something. I didn't want to fail. I'd go through my to-do lists for work and home while in bed. It was draining and I was burned-out.

When I was thirty-four, I decided to leave my corporate career and start my own businesses. Yes, businesses, plural. I was doing portrait photography and making greeting cards while starting a marketing consulting business. I was a one-woman show for both. It was overwhelming while trying to manage a family and a household. Aptly, the photography business was named Busy Bee Studio. Lori was the busy bee buzzing around doing, doing, doing. I can see now I didn't know how to function when I wasn't in this state. It was foreign for me to be still and I had to fill any kind of lull in my life.

When my mom passed in 2007, I jumped in where I felt most comfortable. Getting stuff done. Being her only child, I was the one to take care of her house, belongings, memorial, and Celebration of Life. After these activities were done, many people suggested I go back to work. They said it would be a good distraction from grief. But I didn't accept this concept. Why wouldn't I want to grieve? To me, grief was honoring my mom and the shared connection we had. If I distracted myself to act like it didn't happen, it would be disrespecting our relationship.

I am not one to run or hide from my feelings, so I didn't want to distract myself. I wanted to feel it. I wanted to heal. Up to this point in my life, talking to other people about my feelings had helped me process what I was going through and come out the other side more resolved. Grief brought up so many feelings I had never encountered, and I knew it was going to take time for me to heal. I happened to be ending a three-year contract for work, so the timing was absolutely right to stop working. I can see now what a blessing this was. As for the photography and cards, it became less important. The focus was now on healing—honoring my grief and going through it the best way I could. There was definitely "doing" during this time, but "being" rose to the surface as what I needed: focusing on family and my healing, not working or accomplishing goals. When you lose a loved one and you are consumed with grief, you can also lose your ego and begin to awaken to higher things, like living in the moment. The moment is all you have. You realize saving your happiness for the future is not an option.

For the next sixteen months, I didn't work. It was the first time in my life I chose not to work. I was able to have this luxury because of my mom's life insurance and retirement. Being a mom with two busy kids and focusing on safe driving efforts while grieving was more than enough to keep my plate full. I allowed myself the time and permission to fully grieve the loss of my mom. I was able to follow my intuition on my healing journey. Doing for doing's sake was depleting, but intentional action was rewarding. A little more being, a little less doing, and more intentional action was my home healing remedy. It was the balance I was seeking. In the following chapters, I'll share with you some of my actions, being moments, and healing happenings along my journey.

CHAPTER 4:

Book It, Baby

*"In the case of good books, the point is not to
see how many of them you can get through,
but rather how many can get through to you."*
—Mortimer J. Adler

Reading was a close friend of mine after my mom died. I turned to books for answers, new insights, and to hear stories and get connected. I had my nose in a book a great deal at the beginning. Books offered me an escape from my life. They were a luxurious indulgence from my monkey mind that I couldn't quiet on my own.

A copious number of the books I read were about grief, the majority of which were nonfiction with the author's story of healing from a significant loss in their life. There were also spiritual books, where I found Buddhism to be earnestly insightful, especially when it came to the subject of suffering. I read about how our desire for something to be other than it is leads to our human suffering. I had a strong desire for my mom to still be alive and to put an end to my sadness. I suffered day in and day out, wanting my life to be different. At some point I had to accept that she was not coming back, and that I was going to be gravely sad. Sad for as long as it took. I read everything anyone offered me. I was on the lookout all the time for good books. I was a sponge for information that could help me process and heal my heartache. Since I was looking, things would show up. That's how the world works. What you pay attention to grows. I was paying attention to grief and how to heal, and solutions presented themselves, and I was grateful.

How I make sense of the world around me is by researching and ascertaining how others before me have found success. They have already paved the road, and learning from others is an easier go than trying to pave new ground myself. I could see myself in others and it was comforting. Other people's stories offered me a way to not be alone. They had suffered and were offering their life's canvas as a way to see the world. I could take from it what was right to me. What felt befitting was being in my grief, acknowledging it, then processing my emotions the best way I was equipped.

I love to read, so turning to books to make sense of my situation was a logical choice. This was not always the case. I was not a bookworm as a youngster. I'd read for school projects because I had to. There was an overabundance of reading in college and much of it was boring to me—all those reams of historical nonfiction about politics. It wasn't until I was out of college, when I had the freedom to choose what I read, that I grew to love it. I appreciated how reading broadened my horizons, took me away from my own life, and united me with others. These days I listen to audiobooks while on walks or read my Kindle in bed. The subject matter is all over the map, from memoir, to mystery, to spiritual books. I get excited when I unearth information about people, places, history, technology, new ways to age, and more.

Reading may or may not be your cup of tea. Maybe you'd prefer listening to a book or watching a show. I like to mix it up and dabble in different mediums depending on my mood. I tend to go through phases when I read a lot and then I don't. Ultimately, what draws me in is the story, and stories come in bounteous forms—podcasts, movies, plays, songs, and even YouTube videos. How do you find information that resonates with you? Do you like to listen while you drive, or do you read on your phone, or watch shows on your tablet device? Find your medium and let it flow. It may become one of your best friends you look forward to getting together with every day. I like snuggling on the couch with a cozy blanket, sipping a warm drink, nibbling on my number one nosh, and taking in a story.

CHAPTER 6:

Legend Has It

"Tell the story of the mountain you climbed. Your words could become a page in someone else's survival guide."
—Morgan Harper Nichols

Communication is what connects us, whether it be sending texts, meetings at work, talking on the phone to friends, or meeting up for a meal with family. We do it all day. I know when I am out of touch with people for an extended period of time I am lonely. I also know poor and inauthentic communication can leave me feeling empty. In any relationship, communication is key, including the one with yourself. What are you telling yourself in your head? What is your mind saying?

It is inherent in us to want to connect and tell stories. From the beginning of time indigenous people used petroglyphs, pictographs, hieroglyphics, dance, and music to communicate. When you have a voice, you can hear and see. You don't think about how difficult it would be to correspond without these, if you had no language to share. I am in awe of people with disabilities and all the many ways human beings have or find to connect. We have sign language, braille, alphabet eye blinking, and talking with computers, all in the name of connection. Solitary confinement is a punishment in prison because humans desire and need to relate. It is vital to our growth and well-being.

Each one of us is sharing or hearing stories every day. The simple question of "How was your day?" starts a conversation and then a connection. Turn on the radio and you'll hear stories in the form of news. Watch a movie—a tale someone has brought to life in visual form. A book is story in written form. A song is a story with music and lyrics. Instagram, Facebook and Snapchat are all vehicles for us to share. The list goes on. We are surrounded by storytelling.

When you are grieving, it helps to tell your story. Sharing is caring—caring for yourself as an individual and for the listener. When you share, there is potential healing for both you and the person you're sharing with. To be open and communicate your situation can make you feel vulnerable, and it's a place many choose not to go. For me, it was a necessary part of the healing process. Opening up to people led them to be open with me. Stories start mind to mind and end up being heart to heart.

There are innumerable commonalities in our human lives. Finding out another person's fears, and what helped them through their struggles and even their breakthroughs. We do this through story. It couples our experience. We can pull gems out of shared experiences that resonate with us. We never are really alone. We are all connected. The more we share, the more connected we will feel.

All that is left when we leave this earth are the stories others tell about us—who we were, what made us light up, what made us cry, how we showed up for others, and hopefully the positive impact we had. In the Landmark Forum it's all in the share, as they say. All the participants in their workshops share their lives with one another, and this is how the curriculum is assimilated. The instructor could teach us about integrity, but that's not the point. You get something much deeper when someone's share grabs you. You relate to what another person went through. You see yourself in them. This is mighty compelling.

I had a plentiful number of "signs," as I call them, to share my story. I recognize the synchronicity of my thoughts with what I see in the world. They often align. When you're paying attention, you see more synchronicities. One of the most moving events was at a play Dylan and I attended at the Seattle Children's Theater a year after my mom died. I had season tickets and would take one of the boys to a play and then we'd go out for dinner or dessert afterwards. This was paramount mother-son, one-on-one time. After my mom died, I made a point of planning time together, realizing how important these connections were for me and my sons. Each of them needed special time to nurture our relationship, without the presence of their sibling. The play was called *According to Coyote*. It was about storytelling, an age-old tradition among Native Americans. Gene Tagaban was the one-man show and his message moved me to tears. What he was telling us came from his heart and soul. He closed with these words: "Life is a story. Tell your story. You are a storyteller." His words rocked me to my core. I am grateful to this man, as his play inspired me to keep telling my story and healing. I journaled my story, spoke my story, and wrote my story. I have left a trace of my story for my own healing, but also in the hopes that others will find they are not alone.

As hard as it may be to share your story, the sheer act of telling it will release it from your body and free you from the burden of keeping it to yourself. Ahh, freedom. What a gift!

CHAPTER 7:

Kinship Comfort

"Hearts united in pain and sorrow will not be separated by joy and happiness. Bonds that are woven in sadness are stronger than the ties of joy and pleasure. Love that is washed by tears will remain eternally pure and faithful."
—KHALIL GIBRAN

Grief is a club that no one plans to join or wants to be a member of. I didn't sign up for it, but I did partake, and me and the members of my intimate circle were better off because of our shared reason for joining. We loved my mom, Kathy.

When my mom died, we received many sympathy cards, meals, flowers, emails, and phone calls with condolences. It was comforting knowing people cared and offered their well wishes for me and my family. An interesting thing happened during this time. I discovered that I had expectations for how people should act, and what they should do and say. These expectations inevitably led to disappointments. I believed certain friends should show up for me and offer continued support. Where were they? I discovered along the way that you should never "should" someone. I was sad and couldn't conceive of why people weren't checking in on me. Didn't they understand that I was in a terribly dark place and needed them? Grief can be so isolating.

This was my first adult grieving experience and I didn't know people were so uncomfortable reaching out when someone has died. I've since figured out; it forces others to look at their own mortality and who wants to look at that head on. We know we can't avoid it, but we will surely try our darndest. Many people don't know what to say, so often they don't say anything. In my experience, it's better to say something, even if it is awkward. What you convey to someone who's gone through a loss needn't be eloquent, or even more than a nod or a slap on the back. When there is no acknowledgment, there's a huge elephant in the room, dressed in a fluffy pink tutu, brandishing a diamond tiara and sporting bright pink lipstick. There is no way both parties don't know it's there. As the one grieving, you are waiting for something to be said. You might be left wondering what is so hard for the other person. You may try to mentally coax them, hoping your telepathic thoughts can get them to say, "I'm sorry for your loss." That's it. That's all it would take for the uncomfortable silence between you to vanish into thin air.

While grieving, I had an epiphany. The world didn't revolve around me and it didn't stop because my mom died. Indeed, it kept right on going. It was eye-opening and infuriating at the same time. My world fell to pieces and I wasn't sure it could be put back together. The sun still came out, the seasons arrived, people kept going to work, they laughed and went about their lives. We are all selfish beings, and this was a big dose of reality for me. Just because my world had been altered immensely didn't mean theirs had. In fact, they had their own trials and tribulations going on and lives to attend to. I couldn't take it personally. I also figured out people are more inclined to reach out or offer help when they've been through a hardship themselves. We don't know what we don't know.

I came to a point where I embraced who showed up for me. They came with what they were offering and I accepted. I no longer wondered why certain people hadn't called me or checked up on me. I was thankful for those directly in front of me and present. Being open to what is, and not wanting things to be different, is freeing. You can be more in the moment and surprised by what's in front of you. Buddhism asserts that our desires delude us. If we want things to be different, we feel a continual sense of loss. In that scenario, we're always in grief. Ugh. That sounds awful.

I formed some new relationships which were extremely supportive when I needed them the most. One of those friends was my housecleaner and family friend, Jackie. She's twenty-two years older than me and we formed a close bond during this time, and are still close today. She was an elder who would listen, offer sage advice, and who spoke to me about her spiritual path. I'd never had a friend like her. Looking back through my journals I can see she was a constant in my life, unfailingly there for me when I needed her. Most of the time I vented, expressed my sadness, or just told her about my day. She became the person I'd turn to, like my mom had been, when I needed to talk. She was a great listener, and I am deeply thankful for her support all these years.

I also became closer to a neighbor of mine, Susannah. She had visions of my mom after she died. My mom came to her several times and Susannah would tell me about these visits and the messages my mom conveyed to her to deliver. I found this fascinating, as I hadn't personally known someone who'd experienced this before. We would take walks and talk. We saw the medium John Edward when he came to Seattle. I appreciated her worldview and connection to the supernatural and otherworldly. She was open to numerous ways of living and seeing the world. It was just what the doctor ordered.

Early on I formed two close friendships I would have never expected. My mom's friend Kim and my mom's long-time boyfriend Dave. We had the love and loss of my mom in common and were able to talk about her in ways others couldn't. We missed her so and wanted to observe her presence. We got that from each other by reminiscing about her essence, her mannerisms, funnyisms, how she spoke, what a great friend she was, and her love of animals. Kim and I often shared our dreams with each other where my mom was the main character. Dave told me about a year after she passed that he sensed my mom's presence around him all the time. He felt like she was helping him not be so angry about the situation. He thanked me for including him in the memorial garden and talked about us being family to him. I told him I felt the same way. We both cried and consoled each other. Kim and Dave are still important threads that keep me woven to my memories of my mom.

In addition to my mom's friends, there was something genuinely sentimental about sharing memories of her with my own friends, ones I'd grown up with, who knew my mom when we were kids. They expressed such loving and thoughtful sentiments about her. They told me how sweet and kind and what a fun person she was. It is a unique bridge I share with these friends today, and a place where I can reminisce about her funny voices and uncensored silliness. She lives on in us, and for this I'm so grateful. There were many others who were there for me at that time, too, including my friends, family, and my mom's friends and coworkers.

One afternoon while writing the book, I was on a hike with a friend at Bowman Bay in Anacortes, Washington. We walked along the beach toward Lighthouse Point. As he stopped to stack some rocks, I explored what had washed ashore: clam shells, driftwood, rocks, and seaweed. Then I came upon some Bull Kelp. It is a common sight to see entangled in bunches, but I revel in this ocean treasure because I think of them as mammoth alien seeds that didn't get delivered to their desired destination. They are brownish-green in color, with a bulbous air-filled bladder called a float and a long stem-like structure called a stipe that looks like a whip. As a kid I loved to stomp on the floats, hoping to get a pop and a burst of water out of the bulbous blob.

What caught my eye on that day was the holdfast, the plant's anchor to the ocean floor. The seaweed absorbs nutrients and sunshine from their leaf-like blades which stretch out through the water. This got me thinking about nature and the symbiotic relationships created to ensure our ecosystem remains alive and well. Many living creatures' existence intimately depends on the kelp forest—sea urchins, sea otters, many species of fish, sponges, and invertebrates. When I turned my attention to the forest in front of us, I could see the union between the trees, plants, moss, fungi, birds, and squirrels. Nature demonstrates from sea to land how we need each other to survive. In order to live in harmony, cooperation and a reliance on others is key.

Humans need each other, too. We are each other's ecosystem. Especially in times of grief. Our survival depends upon our relationships with others. We all need people who will listen, console us, offer their support, and ultimately feel a bond with us. I can see how the loving and supportive relationships I've nurtured throughout my life have kept me grounded and provided the ballast necessary to endure hardships along the way. If I didn't have these tethers I would die on the vine. Relationships do require care and feeding to be healthy. They are a partnership. Symbiosis, which means "together" and "life," is a way to look at how we can thrive together. In order for human roots to anchor and "live together" to be mutually beneficial, people must be open to sharing themselves, open to giving to another, and open to receiving in times of need. In the harmonious relationship, there's vulnerability and trust. My grief journey opened my eyes to the importance of relationships. In the end, that's all I care about. Because what else is there?

Be open to who shows up in your life. They are there for reasons you may not deduce at the time. Don't be disappointed by who you expect to show up and how you expect them to act. Trust who is present in your life, and trust that the people who show up for you are there for a reason, and often their purpose is something bigger and better than you can even imagine.

CHAPTER 8:

Show Me a Sign

*"Learn how to see. Realize that
everything connects to everything else."*
—LEONARDO DaVINCI

I was desperate to connect with my mom. Our relationship ended so abruptly, and I was heartbroken. I'd look for signs she was still with me. I'd see or hear something and ask myself, *Was it a sign from my mom? Is she connecting with me? Is she letting me know she's okay?*

I'd heard that signs of someone's presence from the beyond often came in the form of electrical events, sightings, or even smells. I was on the lookout and I did experience some of these occurrences. I am not sure if these were actual signs from her, but at that time the fact that they could be signs from her made me feel closer to her, and that was acutely important for my sanity. Believing she could still be a witness to my life gave me some serenity.

One night shortly after she passed, Jon and I were awakened to the TV blaring in our rec room. It was so loud it even woke up Riley and Dylan who slept like logs. That had never happened before, and never happened since. A clock my mom had given us did the same thing one night. The alarm went off and we had never set it. A light turned on in the motor home about five minutes after we went to bed one night. One afternoon I was leaving the medical examiner's office after picking up some of my mom's belongings and my car sensor started beeping. There was no reason for that to happen. Riley had a small pinball machine that started making sounds spontaneously on several occasions. I shared with my boys that these could be signs from Grama Kath. Whenever something like that happened, Riley would tell me about it and we'd smile, laugh, and hug. It was nice to share in this wondering and belief with my boys. Whatever the explanations might be, the experiences made us think about her in a loving manner.

There were a few times while I was in my house when I thought I saw something out of the corner of my eye. I'd look again and there was nothing there. Repeatedly, I'd wonder if it was her, or whether I was just manifesting my deepest desire. While out and about I'd see women who looked so much like my mom I was sure she was alive and well for a brief moment. I knew it couldn't be, but those experiences sure made my stomach jump and wonder, *What if?* What if this were all a horrible dream I would wake up from and she'd still be alive? I'd often wish that were true.

My mom loved animals and I was drawn to hummingbirds after she passed. As a totem animal they represent messengers, timelessness, healing, warrior, energy, vitality, infinity, affection, and playfulness. My mom's longtime boyfriend Dave was next door working on my neighbor's tree when a hummingbird came right up to my office window. I couldn't help but think of my mom saying, "Hi you two, I see you."

I told Susannah about my encounter with birds and how I felt they were connected to my mom. I proceeded to tell her about the hummingbird that came to the office window in September. Not two minutes later a hummingbird came to the kitchen window where we were standing. We were in awe. How could this be? Was it coincidence, or was it her?

Right after we bought the cabin in Eastern Washington, Jon and I were out on the deck having our morning cup of coffee. A hummingbird flew onto the deck. It stopped, turned to face me, and just looked at me, beating its little wings. Wow! It stayed there for a while as if to say, "I see you. I am happy for you." It stayed long enough to seem extremely intentional about the path it had taken and what it was doing. Jon was equally in awe of this encounter. I was grateful for the visit and said aloud, "Mom, I know it was a message from you and thank you for delivering it in a way that made sense to me."

We kept most of my mom's belongings in a storage unit in hopes we would be able to use them one day. Our dream was to buy a place where we could get away from the city together as a family. Three years after my mom passed, we were able to purchase a cabin with the insurance money from the crash that killed her. We filled the cabin with her furniture and belongings. The essence of her was there. It wasn't a shrine, but it was like an homage to her. The reason we had this cozy and comfortable chalet in the first place was because she was no longer here. We couldn't have bought it on our own. There were carefully collected dishes and artwork she had handpicked and bought over the years from artists she loved at art festivals. Decorative pillows and everything from towels to candles to adorn our new dwelling. It was a blessing to be able to buy the cabin in such a serene location and make use of all her belongings. I thought she'd be delighted about this and the visit from the hummingbird affirmed it for me. Another coincidence: one of the couples we bought it from were named Larry and Kathy. My parents' names. Seemed like a sign to me!

One day at the cabin, a mighty dragonfly with transparent wings, a colorful body, and spherical-looking eyes passed by and it felt again like my mom was sending me a message. My mom had an outdoor piece of white clay art with a raised dragonfly sculpted on it. I saw it every time I went out to our shed where it hung to welcome me on my way to grabbing a garden tool or to get digging in the dirt. When we made steppingstones to honor her memory, I carefully designed my mosaic tiles to construct a frog and a dragonfly. This sits in my yard to this day. Whenever I see a dragonfly, I imagine my mom flying around to be near us. Free.

One night I got up from bed to get a drink of water and smelled perfume. It was like someone was there in the bedroom with me right by my dresser. This happened a second time, too, when I was in bed and I smelled a clean, fresh scent, like soap, right under my nose, and it wasn't the smell of our usual detergent. About a year after my mom died, Jon and I started couple's therapy. In one of our sessions I'd been plugging in with my dad and uncle. I felt the smell could have been one of them. My uncle had a clean and fresh scent. Like the smell of laundry soap on a recently washed shirt. Maybe he'd decided to pay me a visit. I wondered if it was my attention to thinking about him that brought him to me, whether it was his spirit. As with my mom, I didn't care whether these experiences were real or not. I was just happy to be thinking about my uncle regardless of how he appeared.

We had a number of water problems at our house starting about a year after my mom died and lasting roughly six months. First something happened in Riley's room. We had a downpour of rain and our gutters went underground near the house. The water seeped into Riley's room and ruined the carpet. I smelled something a little funky one morning and then confirmed the issue when I reached for something under his bunk bed and it was wet. Not a good sign when the room is fully carpeted. The downstairs bathroom had a similar issue. The gutter going into the ground couldn't handle all the rainwater and neither could the wall of the bathroom. Luckily, we were remodeling the bathroom at the time and easily fixed it. It would have been a real bummer to remodel it and then have the water issue. We ended up rerouting all our gutters from being underground to above ground. This is a Seattle homeowner's issue you must contend with, especially in older homes when the gutters were routed underground right near the house.

Then there was the soffit downstairs leaking from the dishwasher upstairs and some pipes above a storage area. These needed our plumber to come out and put in some new pipes. It was hard to believe we could still have more issues, but we did. Our upstairs bathroom shower enclosure was seeping into the wall and we had to replace it. The p-trap under the bathroom sink was a simple fix, but also qualified as a water issue. It had dripped all over my jewelry boxes.

I read *Sage-ing While Age-ing,* by Shirley MacLaine, in which she shared a time when she was crying and sorrowful and she knew her house felt it. It manifested in her home having wads of water issues—like what we were experiencing. Like her house, our house was undergoing a collective sadness and weeping. There was a stockpile of sadness in our home.

Whether or not you believe in signs, spirits, or ghosts, your heart desires connection and it may look for signs as I did. I don't know if any of these occurrences were my loved ones communicating with me—and that's not the point. The signs united me with them, and it warmed my heart every time. When you are grieving you will take any ounce of joy you can get. Especially when you can reflect lovingly about the person who is no longer there.

CHAPTER 9:

M & Ms
(Mediums and Meditation)

"When you are sorrowful look again in your heart,
and you shall see that in truth you are weeping
for that which has been your delight."
—KAHLIL GIBRAN

A medium is an "intermediary" between the spirit world and ours. Mediums mediate communication between spirits of the dead and the living. People go to them hoping to connect with loved ones who have passed away. For me, this offered something to look forward to, some hope my loved ones were still linked to me and maybe even an afterlife. It was also a welcome distraction from reality, which was death. It helped me get through my grief. It was the honey lemon elixir I was craving.

My mom believed in the paranormal and the possibility of something beyond what we can see and hear, so I believed she may have been inclined to communicate with me as a spirit in this way. Before she passed, I would watch *Crossing Over* with the medium John Edward, and the TV series called *Medium* starring Patricia Arquette. Both were fascinating to me. Could people actually get messages from the dead?

Before my mom died, we talked on the phone every morning. I would get the kids off to school and start working from home, chatting to her from my kitchen landline. She'd be in her office at work in downtown Seattle in the One Union Square building. I was expecting her to come to our house the afternoon she was hit, and so the abrupt and traumatic way she passed left me languishing for answers and some peace. I wanted her to know how much I loved her, how important she was to me, and I wanted to honor her life in purposeful ways. What did she want from me? How could I help her cross over in a loving manner?

One of my first experiences with a medium was when I went to see John Edward at the Washington State Convention Center with Susannah a few months after my mom died. It was a big venue with rows and rows of people like me seeking contact with loved ones. I was disappointed not to receive any kind of reading, but it was clear all people had the same universal question. Edward opened the show with these words: "You all want to know your loved ones are at peace, they are still with you, they are witnessing your life, and that you love them, correct?"

Yes! He hit the nail on the head. This is what I was longing for—to connect with my mom so she knew I loved her. Looking at John Edward's busy tour dates then and now, it's clear that there are a myriad of people like me seeking answers all over the world. This will never cease as we all are going to die one day and leave behind those we love.

A couple weeks after that show, I was contacted by Dave's youngest sister Jean. She told me that my mom had come to her with a message for me: "Your mom loves you. You don't need to die in a violent crash, and she is still a witness to your life." Wow! All of what I was wishing to hear from her. Jean practically sounded like a medium! After that experience, she gifted me a visit to see a local medium named Marie Manucheri. I was touched by her generosity and set up the appointment for five months out since she was booked up to that point.

While waiting for the appointment, I was referred to another medium by Susannah's piano teacher. She had lost someone close to her and found it helpful to talk to someone. The woman's name was Susan Driscoll. She was located in Maryland and channeled the ancient messenger Martin. This was different from John Edward's technique. He sees symbols and correlates these to things he knows in his life and he talks about what he sees. After the reading with Susan, I was somber because I didn't sense a visit with my mom, but the message from my mom was a powerful one. It just wasn't what I expected. The gist of it was this: "It is time for you to slow down and stop being so busy and reflect on yourself. There's something to come out: the true you, the authentic you."

Expectations can lead to disappointments, but it's hard to rid ourselves of them. At the time, I was welcoming more quiet into my life. I knew what I had gleaned from the call with Susan was true. It was time for me to pause and take a new path in life. What the path was at the time I was not sure, but I was on it, so that's what I did. I started slowing down and being more contemplative.

I began meditating for the first time in my life, both to calm my mind and to see if I might have some kind of spiritual relatedness with my mom. I wondered if I might be able to experience an epiphany about life, or become an enlightened being. That was a tall order from a novice meditator, or anyone for that matter. But I was open to a great deal of newness at that time. I had nothing to lose. I had already lost so much.

It's not unusual to be going along with your life and think you have some sense of control only to have the sudden realization you can't control anything. At that point, you either open up or close down. I chose to open up. I tried new avenues, read books, and was vulnerable with my heart. I thought meditation might help stop all the swirling thoughts in my head, or at least redirect them. In truth, getting quiet highlights all the thoughts you have in your mind. Something you find out right away when you sit and are quiet with yourself. Being able to let the thought come and then go with each breath helps you to not go down the rabbit hole with that thought, or make up new thoughts about that thought. What if I do this? How can I fix that? Why am I thinking about this now? This was all new for me.

Meditation was a good exercise in *being* and not *doing*. Doing keeps you busy so your deeper thoughts can be put on the sidelines while you are distracted. I would often meditate when everyone was out of the house, or asleep. The house was quiet, and no one could interrupt me. I found it humorous and a tad frustrating every time I got quiet that our dogs would come up and nudge me and want my love. What was that all about? Maybe the stillness had them wondering if something was wrong with me. I never had an epiphany, enlightenment, or a spiritual kindling with my mom, but meditation did help me explore how to be still, and when a thought came, how to let it go. I was learning to stop the monkey mind from making me crazy. I stopped meditating after a while, but I still practiced letting thoughts go and not churning on them. Today I find walking to be my meditation. Being outside and getting physical activity calms me. My body, mind, and spirit come together when I am in nature walking.

Today, I have more compassion for others, and I am quicker to let things go and not hang on to my ill feelings about people or issues. It is a comfort to notice when this happens, evaluate it, and let it go. Not to get stuck and have these thoughts consume me. Because if they do, it doesn't leave room for higher-level consciousness, like compassion, tranquility, and contemplation.

My session with Marie brought a welcome message from my mom: "Play and have fun." She recognized that my mom would have liked to have been more playful. When I was working on her memorial garden plaque, I brought this message into the poem I wrote called "A Mother's Message." The poem came to me as what my mom would want to say as she reflected on her life, as a message for me and her grandsons. I took a Bridging Worlds class from Marie a couple months later and did a grounding exercise. During that exercise, my Grandma Flo came to me and hugged me and said she was sorry. I'd been so focused on my mom that it was nice to get this from her. She'd died just a little over a year before my mom. Her wish was to not have any kind of memorial, so my mom honored her wish and did nothing. This troubled me, however, as I wanted closure. A memorial is for the people left on earth who loved the person who died. It's a time for those people to come together, to tell stories about the person, laugh a little, cry a little, and console each other. It's a time to bond over our connectedness of knowing this human being who touched us in some way. When this didn't happen, something felt unfinished to me. Now I was finally able to get some closure with my grandma, whose ashes and keepsakes had been passed on to me. I took her ashes to a mausoleum in Wenatchee as she requested. My grandma's nephew Greg met up with my family there. We placed some photos of her loved ones—her two children, Kathy and Rick, and one of us—into a glass case along with her urn. She would have liked that.

A year after my mom passed, Jon, me, and the boys took a trip to New York and Vermont. Susannah grew up in New York and had a family cabin in Vermont. She offered up some New York travel tips, and we stayed with her in the one-hundred-year-old cabin. One night we slept on the porch outside during an electrical storm. I had never seen a storm with lightning of this magnitude. It was scary and exciting at the same time. We don't get lightning like that in the Pacific Northwest. Jon and I had a reading scheduled with George Anderson, a famous medium who's written several books with over a million copies sold. I was going big time with George. I believed the more experienced and the more expensive the medium, the more illumination I would receive. Here's the message that came through from my mom from him: Lori's life has been a Greek tragedy, but that is over now. She said I'd come a long way. I was more in balance. Less anxious. George said my Grandma Flo complimented me on this as well. I believe this was saying to me that I had a lot of sadness in my life from the previous car crashes and family deaths and it didn't need to be this way any longer. Jon was given a similar message. He'd come a long way and was more balanced, too. Pets have been Jon's salvation at times in his life. They are his therapy. They always made him feel better. The message about pets for Jon rang true to me. He would turn to our dogs when he needed comfort, love, and affection. He seemed more connected to them than people when he was sad.

Some accurate messages came from my family through George, but I didn't get specific details to convince me that mediums are absolutely communicating with the deceased. I spoke to my friend Jackie about this and she put it simply: "You still want a relationship with your mom, and you're seeking this through mediums." Exactly. I wanted her back so badly, I'd do anything to have her back. I was clearly in the "bargaining" stage of grief. I also knew that life is too short to be unhappy. I needed to find some solace in life to be there for my sons. That's certainly a lesson hammered into my brain with the loss of my mom. It became harder for me to be around people who were negative or didn't bring me joy. It wore too heavy on my heart. Negativity was a big waste of my precious time here on earth.

Shortly after we got back from our trip to New York, Jon and I started couple's therapy, which we'd continue for four years. It didn't save our marriage, as that ended in 2015, but it did help us understand our issues and communicate about them. Our therapist, Christina, was nonconventional and had a focus on spiritual counseling. She practiced astrology, shamanism, Native American spiritual traditions, ancestral healings, and family constellations, to name a few. Before she became a therapist, she had been a nun and her husband was also involved in her practice by participating in constellations. He was a spiritual healer and nature guide. We were referred to her by one of my close friends who's also a therapist. Her practice was called Hummingbird Spiritual Center, which was perfect. She was just the right mix for us, especially for me since I believed in the possibility of what I couldn't see nor hear. Jon was a sliver more skeptical and more scientific about it, but her conventional counseling style with a dash of the spirituality worked for him.

On one occasion I did a family constellation with Christina and a group of others on a Saturday afternoon. We all were characters, or players, in each other's lives. We'd stand in as someone's mom who'd passed, or whichever relative, to bring the person a message. We embodied the deceased, and it was as if they were talking through you. If nothing came, then nothing came. When it was my turn, my dad showed up and explained how he couldn't know how much he'd affected my mom and me by not being there. His soul saw an ancestor and followed him into death. This man had left his homeland at age sixteen, the same age my dad was when he died. In the session, my mom explained that she kept what little she had of my dad to herself. Even though she had never said this when she was alive, it felt true to me because I never knew much about my dad. She didn't keep his memory alive for me like I would have wished. They weren't together long, and there may not have been much to draw on, but I would have taken anything I could get. I wasn't close to my paternal grandparents. I believe I met my grandpa once and my grandma a handful of times. I am fortunate to have a close relationship to my dad's half-sister, Carolyn. She is ten years older than him, so her memories of him are a bit foggy as she was out of the house when he was growing up.

The overarching message of my constellations were: go to your heart. They are there. To open your heart, you will heal. The greatest contribution my parents gave me was life. I needed to honor it. Later, Christina was a witness and guide in my life during another difficult time I went through—the disintegration of my marriage. She had thought-provoking questions for us to ponder and pushed us to dig deeper as to why we felt a certain way and reacted the way we did. Her nontraditional methods introduced me to a new world of spirituality I hadn't known about before. When I found out that Christina passed away from breast cancer, I considered the impact she had on me, and how the impact we have on others is what is left when our physical life is gone. She dedicated her life to helping others, and I am grateful she impacted mine.

Thirteen years after losing my mom, during the writing of this book, I felt that I could finally interpret what John Edward was saying: "No medium can bring your loved one back. The experience helps, but it isn't the end-all answer. Once you come to terms with never seeing the person again in a physical sense is huge." I see now what I gathered from mediums was beneficial to my healing. Even if there was no concrete evidence, it was a visit or a personal message from my mom, or other relatives. My collective readings helped with my healing. The signs, connections, messages, stories, memories, and time all helped me heal.

CHAPTER 10:

Sleep Sensations

*"A dream is a microscope through which
we look at the hidden occurrences in our soul."*
—Erich Fromm

Dreams can be a way of showing you what you are trying to work through in your awake life. If I write my dreams down after waking and evaluate what is going on in my life, there are many lessons to be drawn. At first glance I often wonder, *How can this dream mean anything?* It might have me in an unfamiliar place, with people I may or may not know. The people I know may be obviously them, but in other ways they're not. It's usually something like, "It was Karen, but she didn't look like Karen." In our dreams, we time travel from one vicinity to the next. After talking about a dream or writing it down, my mind will start to dissect all the pieces. It may not be the people I am thinking about, the situations I am in, or the places they occur, but the feelings are there. Sometimes my dreams reassure me that what I'm wrestling with will all work out as it should. It will all be okay. We process our thoughts about our lives in our sleep, while in an altered state of consciousness. Amazing brains we have!

After my mom passed away, I had an array of dreams about her and was so thankful to have these visions. I was grateful to visit with her. It was her in the flesh talking to me, hanging out with me, and even shopping with me. We were together. It was a place where I could see her face, listen to her voice, and revel in the essence of what made her who she was. I looked forward to sleep and the surprise of being with her while I dreamt.

John Edward did a survey on his show of 25,000 people and asked, "How have those who've passed communicated with you?" The number one response was dreams. I definitely believed my dreams about my mom were another way in which she was communicating with me.

I read a book by Jerry and Esther Hicks called *Ask and It Is Given* in which they write about how what you think about manifests in your life. It is always a vibrational match. Same with dreams—they are a vibrational match. If something manifests in your dreams, it's because you have given it a significant amount of thought. When recalling your dream, take a close look at your feelings. Your emotions give you more important information than the details of the dream. Dreams reflect how you honestly feel and what you're creating. I wanted to create a place where I could spend time and be with my mom. I manifested a slumber-like seventh heaven where things were more colorful and interesting than I could imagine in my awake life.

The first dream I remember about my mom came within a couple months of her death. It was a powerful indicator of how I felt at the time and my perpetual question of: "Was she okay?" The dream's setting was a splendid summer day. My mom was sitting in a rocking chair on the front porch of a cabin in the woods, a flawlessly tranquil setting and in my mind certainly a safe place to be. Then, all of a sudden, a tsunami came crashing toward the cabin. A cresting wall of water was going to destroy her and the cabin. All of this was positively perplexing to me. Where did this unsuspecting raging rush of water come from? She was in the woods. Nowhere near the ocean. It made no sense. There was nothing she could do to escape. She was doomed with no hope in sight and I was a helpless observer. Then she told me she was okay. How could she be okay? She had just been swept away and killed by a tsunami.

When I analyzed the dream, I could see it represented how I thought about the crash and the manner in which she died. I'd been completely blindsided. She was standing on a street corner on a sunny day in June, doing what she had done every day of the week for years: getting ready to cross the street to retrieve her car and head home, in this case to my house. That's when the truck came careening towards her and she was crushed against the utility pole. How could this happen? How could someone run a red light eight seconds after it was red? I was left with unanswered questions. Why did she have to die on this resplendent summer day? Did she see the truck coming toward her and know her fate? I read an eyewitness statement from an onlooker who said they saw her put her arm up as if to shield herself from the oncoming disaster. What went through her mind in that moment? Did she experience pain? How was she now?

The message of "I'm okay" was what I needed to hear at that time. Still, I kept wondering, Was she okay? How did she feel about no longer being alive? Was she angry, sad, or both? Even though the dream was crystal clear about her message to me, that didn't stop me from continuing to seek more answers. This was part of why I sought out mediums—to see if they could tell me the same thing. The fact is that trauma creates these kinds of looping questions that are hard to satisfy. There is no answer, truly, and your brain will attempt to get the same question answered in many different ways. I would continue to seek tranquility within myself on this journey of healing any way I could, but it would take a long time to finally settle into my belief that she really was okay.

I had several dreams after that first one where I found out my mom was alive, and it outright jarred me. In one dream she told me she had been undergoing reconstructive surgeries and had been recuperating at her house. She had a full-time nurse taking care of her. I asked her why she didn't tell me, and she said she wasn't sure she was going to survive and didn't want me to go through her dying twice. The dream made me so sorrowful that she hadn't told me, that I hadn't been there for her.

In another dream she asked me how she'd passed, and I told her the story about the crash, and we sobbed together. In this dream, too, I was alarmed that she was still alive and I hadn't known. I felt guilty about giving her clothes away. I would have never done this if I knew she was alive.

Looking at the feelings in these dreams I can see how badly I didn't want her to be gone. I was still holding out hope she was alive, even years after she passed. I was also clearly unsure if I had done the right thing by giving away so many of her possessions, like her clothes. The guilt I felt over this in real life was spilling into my dreams. Had I done the right thing? She hadn't told me what she wanted done with her clothes and now I wonder why I cared about this so much. I believe it was because she took so much time and care in looking for them and buying them that I wanted to honor her time and attention. She emphatically enjoyed shopping and creating a comfortably chic home and a well-matched wardrobe with just the right accessories. In the end I believe she would have been happy with the time and effort I took to find her possessions a good home, but not that it had caused me so much stress. After all, it was just stuff.

Fear was a feeling I repeatedly felt in my dreams. I was utterly afraid that someone close to me was going to die. Especially my sons. I had several dreams of them dying, as well as others in my life. Most of these incidents were gruesome and involved a vehicle. It was horrible. I'd wake myself up trying to scream or crying and would be so relieved the dreams weren't a reality. I knew from Jon that I would scream in my dreams, which was a call for help where I was essentially yelling, but because it was a dream, the screaming in real life sounded more like muffled and distraught noises to him. Jon coined these noises the screams of "the Witchy Woman." I woke myself up with these screams several times, and always upon waking I was relieved to be out of the unnerving nightmare.

It turns out our prefrontal cortex, which controls reasoning, is dormant when we dream. The parts of our brain activated are the amygdala and hippocampus, which control emotions, so it makes sense that our dreams stir up emotions. When we dream, we are also in a state of paralysis. This keeps us asleep and not acting out our dreams—like running, punching, or kicking.

In one dream I had mimicked my real-life despondency and upset and frustration I had with the driver who killed my mom. In the dream, a truck backed up over Dylan in our cul-de-sac. Oddly, Dylan was not hurt, but the driver would not speak to me. I kept asking what had happened and he was speechless. The driver who killed my mom was also silent on the matter. I never heard a word from him personally, nor through the lawyers. Nothing. In the beginning I coveted a sincere apology, an acknowledgment of what he had done. I desperately wanted a confession of his crime, an admission of guilt, even a hint of grief. I wanted to hear from him that my mom's life mattered and that he was remorseful. I understand why nothing was said due to the legal case, but after it was settled I felt that I should have received something from him. The only thing I read was his statement to the police that he'd gone through a green light. There was no admission of guilt. It took four years to settle and I never heard a word. By that time, I had worked through an ocean of emotions and I'd gotten past the need for an apology. I forgave the driver for his mistake. I don't believe anything he could say today would help me, but I do believe it may help him. Forgiveness sets you free.

Other dreams I had were lighter, where my mom and I would come together in everyday ways, like talking on the phone. We might have a normal conversation where we'd talk about what we did last night and our plans for the day ahead. Or she'd show up at Dylan's baseball practice, or Riley's soccer game, to watch them and chat with me.

In another dream she gave me Prince tickets. She knew he was my favorite and I cherished the surprise gift. In real life, she was a thoughtful gift-giver. She knew just what to give you and was excessively generous. She spoiled my boys to the hilt, and not just on birthdays and Christmas. She loved picking out clothes and bringing over new outfits for them. Toys too, like

Lego sets or the latest Hot Wheels. I missed her gift-giving, and especially the joy it would bring to my boys. To see the excitement and delight it brought Riley and Dylan reflected grandmotherly love and connection.

I am grateful for dreams and the creativity it takes to construct them. I was the artist of these originals and the creations were beautifully branded by my brain. I still dream about my mom, and these sleeping memories and dream experiences bring a smile to my face every time. She will truly be with me eternally.

CHAPTER 11:

Mister Magic

"The song is ended, but the melody lingers on."
—IRVING BERLIN

Music has been a significant part of my life. As a kid I played the clarinet from the fifth to the eighth grade. I wasn't very good, I might add, but in elementary school you chose an instrument and played it during band class. I loved our elementary school assemblies and evening shows where we sang our hearts out. I especially loved the holiday concerts, singing "Jingle Bells," "Up on the Housetop," and "Rudolph the Red-Nosed Reindeer."

Back then we had music as part of our weekly schedule. Singing, that is. We'd go to class and the music teacher would turn down the lights and show us the lyrics of the song on the overhead projector. She'd sit at her piano, sing a song to us, and we'd mimic her. Other times she'd get up in front of the class with her bell-bottomed jeans and long straight light brown hair past her bottom and conduct our symphony of songs. She had such energy and brought pure joy to the class. What a wonderful teacher! I remember the feeling of coming together as one when I'd sing with my classmates. There was a powerful intensity in our togetherness. Our voices sounded better united than as a single songbird. I still know the words to some of those songs today. I invite you to reflect on your childhood memories and see if you can conjure up some ditties.

My boys didn't have a choir class in grade school, though they did have band starting in the fifth grade. It bummed me out, as I had such nostalgic memories of this part of my life. They did partake in singing during preschool and kindergarten, but not so much after that. Their dad and I were on the same wavelength with regards to music. We enjoyed the same artists and genres and listened to music together often, whether in the car on road trips, or while making dinner, or taking in live concerts, or watching music on TV. Music was consistently a part of our life. We introduced music to our sons and shared what we loved. They heard a mélange of music growing up and we went to see a variety of artists perform live. We also gave them music lessons, with Riley starting piano at age five. He played through high school and also took up the drums as his instrument in fifth grade. Dylan wanted to play the drums straight out the gate, so he got lessons as well.

Their dad and some of his friends would come over and jam with the boys in our downstairs rec room. Boy was that loud! Jon would play the drums, Riley the keyboard, and Jon's friends the guitar and the bass, while Dylan would improvise lyrics. He was so darling, a little guy with a big microphone, belting out his own blues lyrics about his dog and what he ate for breakfast that morning. I love watching my sons play music together. There is nothing better than my house being full of music, laughter, and my sons bonding.

Today my sons introduce me to new music. Oh, how the tides have turned. I love their eclectic taste that includes rap, country, EDM, indie, and classic rock. Riley has even made me playlists on Spotify of new music he thinks I'd like. I gravitate toward R&B because it reaches into my chest and tugs on my heart and soul.

My mom's love of music was a big influence in my life, and this informed how I passed music along to my boys. She was regularly listening, singing, and grooving to tunes. She was never afraid to sing in the car or get down when the music moved her. It rubbed off on me. I was born in 1970, so she was playing vinyl albums on the record player and cranking the '70s sounds on the radio station KJR in her Volkswagen bug. She loved Bread, The Doobie Brothers, Cat Stevens, Led Zeppelin, Grover Washington, Jr., and Phoebe Snow, to name a few.

Growing up, whenever I'd get a chance to go to the mall, I'd burn a hole in my pocket and buy a new 45. I still have my records and tapes from that era. Whenever I look at them, it transports me back to that time in my life. I may not always remember the details or the events, but I remember how the music made me feel. I loved making mixed tapes for myself, my friends, and my boyfriends. My Walkman was my best friend as a teen. I could escape into my own world and listen to Prince's *Purple Rain* album, or Depeche Mode's 1985 album, *Catching Up the Depeche Mode,* over and over again. I hear them now and it takes me right back to my teen bedroom where I had Jaclyn Smith photos plastered on my wall. She was from the original Charlie's Angeles trio and my favorite.

My first concert without an adult was Prince's Purple Rain tour. He would become my favorite artist of all time. Prince is in my DNA. I'm fairly certain there's purple plasma pumping through my veins. During the time when I was reading so much following my mom's death, I discovered a term called Identity Development. This is when young people derive a sense of identity from music: when the lyrics speak to them and they identify with what's being said, whether it is about love, loss, or finding oneself. I wonder what changes for us in adulthood, but I certainly know the influence of music from my teen years and how potently powerful it is to me even when I hear that music that informed me growing up.

One of the first events I planned to honor my mom's life and heal my own was her Celebration of Life. This event included a thoughtful selection of music that reminded me of her, played with a slideshow. It was both painful and healing to collect these songs and photos. I was gratified knowing that she would have certainly enjoyed the music. A friend of ours sang Tom Petty's "Wildflowers," and a song she wrote called "Letting Go." She and the guitar player played an enchanting acoustic performance. My mom would have loved it.

A few months after she died, I was at Mom's rental house digging up the dahlia bulbs she'd planted. Her garden was magnificent and her healthy dinner plate dahlias were begging to be in the ground at my house. She took such care in making her home a place of beauty and comfort, inside and out. Selfishly I wanted a piece of her in my yard. I imagined seeing the flowers bloom in the summer and thinking about her love of nurturing a garden. It was a way to honor her memory and keep her alive for me, Jon and the boys. When I finished digging up the dahlias, I climbed into our Yukon XL to head back home.

Of course, I turned on the radio as a car ride is much better with music. The song "Mister Magic" by Grover Washington, Jr. was on the radio. It is a nine-minute soul/jazz instrumental song featuring an album cover with a man emerging from a pool, water dripping down his bearded face. So simple, but memorable. This interlude had me linked to my mom, like she was saying, "I see you."

When my mom died, music played a meaningful role in my continued connection with her. I'd hear a song and it would trigger a memory of her. Especially if it was a song or an artist I knew she liked, or I'd heard her play throughout the years. Sometimes a song would have lyrics, or a melody that made me think of her, a time together, our love, and now my loss. You name it, I felt it. Initially music made me wistful because it exacerbated the loss I felt. I've read about how music therapy can help you process, cope, and walk through your journey of grief. I didn't have a music therapist in my life, but music certainly helped in my own healing. So, turn on the radio, open your app, and listen to some tunes. See how your own experiences can resonate with the lyrics and help give a voice to how you are feeling. Music has some magical properties just waiting to heal.

CHAPTER 12:

Reading with Riley

*"It is the basic principle of spiritual life that we learn
the deepest things in unknown territory. Often it is when we
feel most confused inwardly and are in the midst of our greatest
difficulties that something new will open. We awaken most
easily to the mystery of life through our weakest side. The areas
of our greatest strength, where we are the most competent and
clearest, tend to keep us away from the mystery."*
—JACK KORNFIELD

I loved the bedtime ritual with my boys when they were growing up. I was usually the one to tuck them in each night and
it was our one-on-one time to connect. Typically, we'd start
by chatting about their school day, friends, sports, or music.
Then we'd read a book or two and I'd scratch their backs and
hopefully they'd drift off to sleep. Sometimes the talking would
lead to feelings they needed to express, which could then lead

to deep conversations. I never knew what was going to happen and it was often magical. Being in our pjs all snuggled up was like a cocoon of safety for all the afflictions that were held at bay during the day. They would open up and share their innermost thoughts. My care and affection were paramount in these delicate and vulnerable times.

Around the time my mom died, Riley was reading Hardy Boys books. Brothers Frank and Joe Hardy were teen sleuths solving cases that stumped even the adults in their crime-infested hometown of Bayport. The first three stories were published in 1927 and here we were reading them eighty years later. The style and manner in which they spoke was more formal back then and we got a kick out of the language. We'd take turns reading the pages and Riley would do accents for each of the characters. One night he was doing a New York accent for the character Rumble Murphy and he had me cracking up. Just what I needed at the time. To laugh at such a sad time gave me hope that I may be normal again one day.

Riley's way of offering me support during this difficult time was different than Dylan's. Riley was five-and-a-half years older and they of course had their distinct personalities. Riley leads more with his thoughts and Dylan is more physical. Riley would often know I was sad and just look at me or say something comforting. On the first Halloween without my mom, I told Riley I was carving a pumpkin my mom would like. When I was done, I asked him if he knew what I'd carved in my pumpkin. He said, "It doesn't matter; you and your mom know what it is." His sentiment was just right as my carving skills weren't stellar. I had done my best to carve a frog's face. Two big bulging eyes with vertical slits for pupils, two round holes for nostrils, and a long narrow mouth with a tongue extended to catch its next meal. My mom had a large collection of frog figurines and artwork. Hard to see a frog and not think of her. She'd know what it was.

On the first Christmas after she passed we decided to go to Costa Rica for a change of scenery, thinking it would be too difficult to get through my first Christmas without her. We opened our presents before the trip and I started tearing up. Riley didn't skip a beat and said, "Mom, she's still with us even though we can't see her." These thoughtful responses from him were comforting, and I was grateful for my emotionally aware son and how he was keeping her memory alive for himself.

Keeping a loved one's memory alive is personal to each of us. Our innermost thoughts can conjure up a time we spent with our loved one, a shared meal, a road trip, a concert, or a deep conversation. Objects we have can serve this purpose, too. I have several items in my house that were my mom's, or gifts given to me that remind me of her. There are a lot of objects involving hummingbirds. My mom was a collector of rocks, shells, and other outdoor treasures. She liked to bring a little something home after visiting a new place. Riley went away to sixth grade camp for the week and brought home some rocks. As he was showing them to me, I told him about my mom and how she would do exactly the same thing. It was an important moment, as he was happy to be like his grandma in this way. To this day he is a collector of mementos.

When Riley was twelve, we had a conversation about how my mom, dad, and uncle all died in crashes. We talked about how important family is and not possessions. I told him he was a smart young man and how proud I was of him. He said it was because of his parents. It was in his genes, and we had taught and had shaped him. He commented, "Wasn't it great that you and your mom were so close. She taught you well and you could pass it on to your kids and then we pass it along to our kids."

During those years when I was getting all kinds of signs from my mom, it was Riley I shared with—and he would celebrate with me when these little synchronicities occurred. It was a bond between us that no one else shared.

Riley was an eager helper and I was grateful for his assistance. One day I was gathering up my cards to take to my mom's friend Kim's shop. She had a rubber stamp store where she sold handmade cards. He helped me put the cards in the racks and pack them in the car. He told me how great the cards were and how the borders I chose looked nice with the photos. It was so sweet, and I appreciated the kind words, as my mom was usually the one to offer those. She loved my cards and was a source of encouragement for me.

My sons were a gift to me during my darkest days of grieving. I never expected them to be a source of such comfort. They were children, and my assumption, as I shared earlier in this book, was that the adults in my life would show up for me. That's the rub. Expectation. When you have expectations of people and situations you are likely to be disappointed. I found myself changing to be more open to what was, or what is. No expectations. I often find I am delightfully surprised by what happens with no expectations. The fewer assumptions I have about how I presume a given situation is going to go, the better. That's when the beauty shows up—in the unknown. I can't control how things are going to happen, so resisting is futile. I often look back on situations and see how liberating it is when I've been able to let a situation unfold instead of trying to control it.

CHAPTER 13:

Dancing with Dylan

*"There is nothing as powerful as mother's love,
and nothing as healing as a child's soul."*
—ANONYMOUS

Dylan was six when my mom died, and the depth of his empathy, kindness, and loving heart during that time greatly nurtured my healing. For such a little guy he was so wise and knew exactly what to do and say when I was hurting. He'd give me a hug, ask me to dance, make me laugh, and bestow heartfelt messages at just the right time. There's an expression: "Out of the mouth of babes." This is a shortened and revised expression of the Old and New Testaments of the Bible. In Psalms 8:2, God ordains strength out of the mouth of babes and sucklings; in Matthew 21:16, praise comes from this source. Later generations changed strength and praise to wisdom. In a nutshell, this saying exists because children, though inexperienced, do indeed say wise, insightful, and mature-beyond-their-years things. I was exposed to this firsthand through Dylan.

The bedtime routine, as I mentioned, was a sweet time with my kids. Dylan often had deep questions that he'd pose at bedtime. A few months after my mom passed, Dylan was sad and asked why our dog Abby and Grandma Kath had to die. I don't recall how I answered him, trying to keep what I said age-appropriate. I told him, "We all die at some point;" but I was so raw and didn't want to have an answer as to why my mom had died. I didn't want her to die. I wasn't ready. But I also appreciated him asking. I love that children have no filter. They say what they are thinking. This made me feel that he knew he was safe. I also appreciated that he was not jaded by life, and had no fear of being judged for his thoughts and feelings.

On another night, I was tucking Dylan in and the song "Easy" by The Commodores came on. We'd often listen to mellow music at tuck-in time. He started to cry and said he was thinking about all the good and bad things that had happened to our family. One bad thing he shared was that his older brother had taken apart a Lego set he'd worked hard on. I comforted him by reminding him of good moments we'd had as a family. Then to my surprise he said he wanted to dance with me. We climbed out of his bed and danced in his bedroom. He demonstrated some new moves for us to try. He was a boldly competent choreographer. This helped him feel better, and me, too.

Another night he asked how my mom and dad had died. This question made me cry. My little boy was thinking about how my parents died, and I was sure it was scary for him, especially since I had to explain these two incidents—one with my father falling asleep at the wheel and one with my mom being hit in a crosswalk. As I told him about what happened, I cried.

He stroked my hair. Such a sweet and sensitive little man. At the end of our talk we laughed together when he noted that my mom was very young to have a baby at nineteen. He was right! When Dylan was almost seven, he expressed, "My heart was made for dancing." I told him, "My heart was made for loving my family." At the writing of this book, Dylan is eighteen and I would love to have this exchange with him today. As a young adult he's more inhibited, as most of us are. Why do we lose our capacity to express? I know I lost it for a while, and it came back in my middle age years. I love to dance and don't care what anyone thinks of my moves, or lack thereof. It is more important for me to explore the freedom dancing brings than care what anyone else thinks.

When I was growing up, I'd spend weeks with my Grandma Flo in the summer. She and my grandpa divorced when my mom was sixteen. The story was that my grandma had turned bitter afterward and was a man-hater. I don't believe this, but I do believe she was devastated by her husband leaving her for a woman twenty years younger. This made her guarded. If you were in her circle, you were loved and well taken care of. I knew she was solidly in my court. If you weren't, she was wary of you and it took a good deal for her to warm up.

There was one area of her life where I saw her light up, though, and that was when she danced. She would often grab me and we'd dance around the living room, or in the kitchen. She'd twirl me this way and that. She'd smile, laugh, and hum a tune. It was always unexpected when she'd do that. I loved it! She did this with my boys, too. I wish she were alive today so we could share our love of dancing. I'd love to ask her about her favorite dances, hear about her dance partners, and we could swap some moves with each other.

My mom was no stranger to letting loose and being goofy. She'd crank up the tunes and jump and jive around the house—uninhibited, silly, and festive. I tend to get fantastically frivolous when I dance, too. I love to make up moves and give them names, like the butterfly, the pepper grinder, or the karate chop. In the fourth grade one of the teachers taught us how to square dance. We'd go to the gym, master our moves, and put on performances all dressed up in our outfits. I remember wearing a skirt and vest my grandma made for me. Here's the Barn Dance Heel Toe Polka we perfected: Heel and toe, heel and toe, slide, slide, slide. Heel and toe, heel and toe, slide, slide, slide. Clap right, clap left, clap knees, clap both, swing, swing, swing around to a new partner!

It's not a surprise to me that I found dancing to be healing when I was grieving. *The Oprah Show* was a favorite of mine during that time. I remember one episode where Gwyneth Paltrow talked about her postpartum depression and explained how she started dancing for exercise. She described how it helped her mind and body come together. It inspired me to dance for exercise, too. I'd go down to the rec room, turn the disco music channel on the TV, and start bouncing to the beats. Some *Saturday Night Fever* John Travolta moves would come over me. I'd point my finger over my head, then swing my arm across my body and down to the ground and back again. I was literally "Staying Alive" with The Bee Gees.

Dylan had a way of reminding me to slow down and make time for love and connection. Like the poem I wrote at the beginning of the book, "A Mother's Message." Be present, be aware. One night he was tired and upset about a playdate he'd had earlier that day. He told me his love tank was empty and had a hole in it. Such a great analogy after a hard time with a friend. I gathered all his stuffed animals, about twenty of them, and placed them around him on his bed. He loved his stuffies. I cuddled up beside him and he fell asleep in my arms. It doesn't get much better than that—being there to help ease your child's suffering, offering love and a warm embrace. Just as he did for me.

To this day, Dylan snaps me out of what I am doing and gets me into love. He helps me to be grateful for being alive and having the family I have. During my healing journey, I started to take his lead and give hugs to those I love for no reason at all. There doesn't need to be a reason to show someone you love them.

One morning not too long after my mom died, Dylan came into the kitchen wearing his Grandma Kathy's "Weiss Tree Service" sweatshirt and exclaimed, "I like to wear this because it smells like Grama Kath. It smells good." I breathed it in as I hugged him. I looked him in the eyes and said, "I miss Grama Kath." He asked if I was crying and I said yes. He said, "I'm sorry, Mom." I told him I was okay. I was happy he had a nice memory of my mom and for his empathy when I was sad. There's such kindness and purity that comes from a child's heart. I was fortunate to be on the receiving end of his love. He didn't try to fix me or tell me to get over it. He just said he was sorry, offered me love, kind words, and a hand for a dance. My dancing Dylan.

Letting love seep into the cracks and crevices of your broken heart is the relieving remedy to mend your wounds. Be open to all the gifts as they appear. A smile from a stranger, a phone call to say hi, a kindred spirit, a dog's nuzzle of their muzzle, belly laughs with friends, remembering a memory of your loved one, and of course a hand for a dance.

CHAPTER 14:

Keen Creatures

"Animals are the bridge between us and the beauty of all that is natural. They show us what's missing in our lives, and how to love ourselves more completely and unconditionally. They connect us back to who we are, and to the purpose of why we're here."
—TRISHA McCAGH

I never imagined my pets would provide me the love I needed when my mom died. It was a welcome surprise. Most of us who have pets are aware of the unconditional love they offer, especially dogs. They're endlessly happy to see you, play with you, cuddle with you, and look at you with those sweet eyes as if to say "I see you."

When Jon and I moved into our first apartment, we got a black and white kitty named Iggy. We hadn't had him for more than six months when someone shot him with a bb gun. Being on a shoestring budget, Jon was able to negotiate a lower price for Iggy's surgery to remove the bullet. We had to keep Iggy inside while he healed, and he was not happy about his limited freedom. When he was well enough to go outside, he never came back. We did see him once on our fence with a red bow around his neck. We guessed he'd decided to find a new home. Probably someone who didn't keep him inside.

After his escape, a friend of ours had a litter of kittens, so we picked a long-haired orange and white one and named him Hector. Hector lived seventeen years and in the three homes Jon and I shared. He was a cleverly cool cat, almost like a dog. When we'd walk to the park with our dog and kids, he'd follow us. I'd worry about him finding his way home, but he never strayed. He was a sweet cat, not aloof like so many cats I've encountered. He could bite you sometimes, but it was more of a love nip. He reminded me to relax and be in the moment. When a feline friend saunters over to you with the intention of sitting on your lap and getting love, you must sit. Sit and be.

Jon and I got our first dog right after we moved into our first home. She was a chocolate lab and we named her Abby (or Abigail Louise). Jon would take her to our nearby park to train her to be a bird-hunting dog. He'd bring pheasant feathers to teach her the scent and get her flushing and fetching. One day at the park she ran off and he later found her with another lab. Uh oh. As her belly started to grow, it was obvious she was pregnant. She and I were pregnant at the same time, in fact. Both of us with our swollen bellies was a vision to behold. She had six puppies, three yellow and three black. Dang were they cherub-like. It was hard not to keep one, but with a baby on the way we decided it would be too much to manage.

When Abby was eleven, around the time Riley was ten and Dylan was four, we got another chocolate lab puppy. We'd heard pups learn from being around older dogs. It was amusing to watch Etta follow Abby around and mimic what she did. Abby practiced a marked amount of patience with Etta, who was under her feet and perpetually ready to play. Abby's health was declining at that time, and it was hard to see her deteriorate. She'd had diabetes for a while and was almost blind at the end of her life. Animals can't tell you how they feel or what they want, so seeing her suffer was difficult.

When my mom passed, she had a deaf six-year-old Jack Russell Terror (oops, I mean Terrier) named Holly. This little twenty-pound pooch was pure spunk. I am not sure what her deal was, but she thought she was an alpha dog. Being deaf made her jumpy and you couldn't let her out of your sight because there was no calling her back. It was nerve-wracking for me. She also seemed to have a death wish. When any sort of truck came by, she'd pull on the leash and dart toward its underbelly. I believe it was the vibration of the heavy truck on the pavement that got her going. It may have been her breed, her personality, or not being socialized with other dogs, but she was a nervous nellie. I've heard dogs take on their owner's temperament. If the owner is anxious, so is the dog. I am not sure if this is a solid theory because we had a chill dog, Etta, and an anxious dog, Holly. I know Holly made me anxious, so maybe it was a circle of unease.

Holly had an irresistible quality I don't encounter much in animals, which is smiling. She would smile sometimes. Especially for Jon and Dave. Since she was deaf, we had a hand gesture we'd do to say hi to her. You'd take your hand and move it sideways as if to say, "Hello. I am happy to see you." She would wiggle her body vigorously and pull her lips back so you could see her teeth and gums. A doggie grin. The last year of Holly's life was difficult for the both of us. She would go to the bathroom in the house and pace in circles walking in her own feces. It was like she had dementia. Every morning I'd spend about an hour cleaning the floor and her. I held on for a long time, not wanting to euthanize her, hoping she'd pass on her own. She was the last piece of my mom and I was holding on tight, but we were both miserable. I was keeping her alive for selfish reasons. I was finally able to let go and take her to the vet. Dylan helped me bury her in the backyard under a large bamboo tree. I am thankful for her sweet stubbornness and the patience she taught me.

My mom also had my grandma's green and yellow parakeet named Pat. We weren't sure how old Pat was, or even its gender. Usually you can tell if they're male or female by their bluish or pinkish color of their cere (the fleshy area above their beak where you see a set of nostrils). Pat had a growth on its cere, hence the name Pat. We welcomed them into the family. At this point we had four pets: Etta and Holly the dogs, Hector the cat, and Pat the bird.

My sadness hung onto me like a tick sucking the blood from its canine host. It consumed me and often I was home alone with the animals. Jon would be at work and the boys at school. I found the animals had a keen intuition and knew when I was hurting. If I was crying on the couch, they'd come sit right under my feet and look up at me or nudge me for pets. They seemed to be able to sense my pain and I felt they wanted to share the burden with me. The push of a wet nose on my hand would get me out of my mind and into the now. I would think about what I was grateful for. Sometimes I'd get on the floor with them; stroke their coats, cry, and talk about my mom. They were adept listeners. No judgment or words of advice, just their presence. That was plenty. They also provided me with some unexpected laughter, like when I would try to meditate and they'd vie for my attention. It's hard to sit and let the thoughts go when you have two dogs licking your hand. I'd move from the living room to the rec room to the bedroom and they'd follow me each place I'd try to sit silently. I'd often give up and start laughing. I guess I was meant to laugh and give them attention in those times. It was rather therapeutic.

About six months after my mom died, I was tucking Riley in when I started to cry. Etta and Holly happened to be on the bed with him. They often traded off sleeping with the boys. It was a silly sight—two dogs on a twin bed with a kid. The dogs would stretch their entire bodies out to get comfortable, not leaving much room for a human. This night Holly licked the tears off my face. She had never done this before, and it was so sweet. It was like she was saying, "I see you are sad. I accept your pain and I want to take it away."

I had another tear-licking incident, but this time was with Pat. Pat and I would whistle to each other back and forth during the day and I would go up to her cage and she would give me kisses with her beak. Yes, I came to refer to her as a girl over time. She just seemed like a girl to me, though I have no clue. One night I was sad and took her out of her cage and was holding her on my finger. As I was crying, she licked my tears off my face with her tiny tongue under her triangular curved beak. In both moments I embraced love from my pets. I was reminded to love. To slow down. To be and just love.

When we were in Costa Rica that first Christmas, we encountered lots of animals. The bungalows where we stayed had oodles of dogs, and cows were everywhere we drove. The cows had large doe eyes and floppy ears. They reminded me of big dogs. I was connected to the animals on the trip. We made friends with some of the bungalow owners and they suggested we go to the rodeo. I was apprehensive about going, as I didn't want to see calves getting roped and people riding bulls. It was cruel to me, but I ended up going anyway. What I saw made me physically sick. I had an affinity with these animals. This was a change in me since my mom died. I looked at everything differently and was more aware and interconnected with my surroundings. I tried to explain this to Jon at the time, but he didn't understand why that meant I couldn't watch the animals at the rodeo. He didn't see it as cruel, but I did. I know I was extra-sensitive to everything at the time, like I had a heightened sense of awareness of everything around me, including animals.

I've mentioned how my mom loved hummingbirds, so when I'd see them, I'd think of her and it would bring me a sense of calm. Hummingbirds are symbols of enjoyment of life and lightness of being. This fascinating bird is capable of the most amazing feats despite its small size, such as traveling great distances or being able to fly backwards. Hummingbirds inspire with their adaptability and resiliency while keeping a playful and optimistic outlook.

I see how my healing journey has built up my resiliency to stress and anxiety while keeping me mindful of being in the now and enjoying life's simple pleasures. All animals I encounter today remind me to cultivate play, joy, and love in my life. I am hard-pressed not to baby-talk to all dogs I see, or give them a pet and kiss on top of their heads. They are so darn precious and full of love to give. I want to take it all in.

CHAPTER 15:

Crying and Laughter Unite

"Within tears, find hidden laughter;
seek treasures amid ruins, sincere one."
—RUMI

I cried a lot when my mom died. It was a torrent of tears, a cataclysm of crying, and I became a woeful weeper for more than a year. I didn't know I could wallow in such anguish. The emptiness inside me literally made my heart hurt. I understood the word heartache on an intimate level. The physical manifestation of grief was real. It was hard to know any kind of normal. My mind was like a record stuck on repeat, skipping in the exact same spot over and over again. Everything I did and everywhere I went I was reminded of my mom. I could not fathom never seeing her again, talking to her, hearing her laugh, or giving her a hug. All those thoughts made me incredibly sad. And when I am sad, I cry.

It was hard to be around other people at times, as I never knew when I'd start crying. I didn't want to make people feel bad, or for them to feel they needed to console me. I felt especially bad for Jon, Riley, and Dylan, since they saw me sad the most. I would literally be okay one minute and weeping the next. I am sure it was hard for them to see me this way and not be able to fix it. The boys were especially good at not trying to fix it. They'd lean in for a hug, a kiss, or say they were sorry. That's all I needed. Someone to see me, acknowledge my pain, and offer me a little comfort. Initially my mom's death brought Jon and I closer together, but as time went on it drove a wedge between us. He was ready for me to be back to normal and I was still deep in grief. I would never be the same again. The loss had stopped my life in its tracks and I was alone on this transformative journey.

If you've ever been profoundly sad, you know that crying is part of the process. You are grieving and the natural reaction is to be sad and cry. At least it is for most people I know. I say embrace it. The only way to heal is to grieve. Pushing your feelings down won't do you any good. If you don't go through it now, you'll have to go through it later. Later may be when you are grieving something else and this piled on top of it could be doubly hard.

I was fortunate to be able to take the time I needed to honor how I wanted to grieve. I was determined to feel it all. Several people suggested I go back to work to distract myself. They said it would take my mind off the loss. I could not conceive of that, however. As I mentioned in the beginning of the book, I didn't want to take my mind off losing one of the most important people in my life. To do that would deny how much she meant to me.

I found crying to be a cathartic release of my emotions and extremely therapeutic. Having a good cry can help you move through what you are feeling.

Crying is a fascinating biological response, since it happens when we're sad, but also when we're happy. We have psychic or crying tears that are produced in response to strong emotions, like stress, pleasure, anger, sadness, and physical pain. Our emotional reactions trigger our nervous system, which in turn activates our tears. These tears contain leucine enkephalin, a natural painkiller. This is part of the reason our mood will be elevated after a good cry. There's another potential reason we cry—to elicit help and support from those around us. When you share a moving moment, you mesh with one another. I can fully relate to this. Crying equals connection.

In the 1980s, biochemist William H. Frey's favorite hypothesis was that stress is bad for the health of the brain, heart, and other organs. His theories suggest that crying likely served humans throughout our evolutionary history to reduce stress. When you cry and get support of others, it is a stress relief. Think of a baby crying to signal they need attention. An adult comes to their aid to end their tears, whether it be to feed them, change their diaper, or soothe them. I know when I cry in the presence of others that I will be better as soon as they have listened to what pains me and communicated that they grasp my situation. I know I am not alone.

At some point during the first year of grieving, I realized suffering is part of living. If you believe you can go through life unscathed, you will indeed suffer more. Accepting that there is suffering doesn't mean you like it, but it does mean your resistance to it lessens. Life's moments ebb and flow. Some days we are on top of the world and full of hope. Other days are exhausting and overwhelming. To know this can ease your mind when you're having the down days, weeks, and maybe even months. The only constant in life is change. The sooner you can be in harmony with this fact, the more at ease you will be.

I look to nature and the seasons as my steadfast examples of change. I know they will consistently occur. Some seasons I like better than others, but I acknowledge they are going to happen regardless of what I desire. I embrace what each of them offers and adapt my life, wardrobe and activities accordingly.

About a year after my mom died, my friend Susannah and I went to a play at the ACT theater. It was in the style of a Greek tragedy. The characters had all lost a loved one and were grieving deeply. To end their suffering, they could wash themselves in the river and no longer remember their past. The hole in their heart was so vast that they were willing to forget the person so the pain would disappear. This spoke to me directly. What would I do if there were a way to end my suffering and not remember a hurt so vast? To be oblivious that someone I loved so vehemently was erased from my memory? Would I trade that to end the ache and emptiness I felt? I concluded that the tradeoff would rob me of what brings me joy and appreciation. In my case, the memories of my mom made me sad because I didn't have her anymore, but I also loved those memories and clung to them, knowing that someone had loved me so deeply, and remembering how much she'd informed my entire life. I reckon you need to be engulfed in the sadness to fully appreciate the love. I like this quote by the prophet

Kahlil Gibran: "Some of you say, 'Joy is greater than sorrow,' and others say, 'Nay, sorrow is greater.' But I say unto you, they are inseparable. Together they come, and when one sits alone with you at your board, remember that the other is asleep upon your bed."

The opposite of crying may be laughing. I love to laugh and welcomed it as an emotional release during my time of grief. There were times when I felt guilty to be laughing, as if I were telling the world I wasn't sad. I was having too much fun for a daughter who'd lost her mom. Of course, that wasn't true, but the mind can tell you some twisted shit. My mom was goofy, so I'd share stories with others about her and we would giggle. She would have loved that. It was glorious to be happy for a moment or two. To step outside of my grieving self to be my happy self again. To get a glimmer of how the future could be as a healed daughter.

Laughing and crying are two activities we do as humans where we can recognize what the person is feeling without speaking the same language, or saying a word to each other. I find this thought-provoking. There are other ways that laughing and crying are similar. Like crying, laughter brings people together. Crying situations offer emotional support and laughing offers social support. Connection and support from others ultimately make us feel better and can improve our mental and physical health. In that vein, laughter may be the best medicine. I dig it!

Did you know laughter is thirty times more frequent when you are with someone else? Laughter creates a bond between us through humor and play. I know the closest friends I have are those I can laugh and cry with. A few months after my mom passed, I was fortunate to participate in some laughing episodes. Once was with two of my friends, Megan and Angela. We were working on the scrapbook from my mom's Celebration of Life and started cracking up about something. The three of us will often do that. We get laughing so hard about something we are all doubled over and crying. It is delightful to be able to laugh this hard with others.

Another person I laugh like this with is my friend Jean. On a drizzly afternoon one November, she and I had met at our usual garden café at Swansons Nursery for lunch. We were both a touch rummy on this day. She had a cold and I had a headache. We started laughing about something uncontrollably. It was like our walls were down and our vulnerability allowed us to open and blossom like fragrant flowers. It's graceful to see vulnerability in another and allow it in yourself. It was healing for the both of us.

A person's laugh is individual to them. Whether it be a high-pitched cackle or a deep guttural groan, you hear it and identify spot-on who the person is. It's like the uniqueness of a person's voice, mannerisms, or handwriting. My mom had the cutest laugh. It delights me to think about her laughing. I read that genes may play a role in your laugh being similar to your parents, but more likely it's that we grow up and hear our parents' laugh and adapt elements of it as our own, as we are a highly imitative species.

My mom was friends with her landlord Lloyd. Lloyd and I were talking a few months after she died to close up some final details, and he asked me if I could help him put some rock music on his new iPod. He said he didn't have a computer and needed some help. I was happy to oblige. He left his iPod with me and came by the house a few days later to pick it up. I started laughing for some reason. He got quiet, took a moment, and said,

"You sound just like your mom when you laugh." I thought he might tear up. When he left I cried. You never know what may come in life. Helping him in turn helped me. It was a bonus to hear that my laugh was like hers, and she lives on in me.

One evening at dinner, Jon and the boys and I went around the table and each said something about my mom. We were all in stitches recalling my mom's reluctance to snorkeling. Or her stronger aversion to getting saltwater in her mouth. My mom had joined us on vacation in Maui when Riley was nine months old. It was the first time to Maui for all of us. She loved lying in the sun and swimming in the water. As a kid I enjoyed watching her swim in Lake Chelan. She'd gingerly get into the cold water until it was up to her waist, then she'd immerse herself, splaying her arms out into a breaststroke. She'd swim out a stretch, all the while trying not to get her face or hair wet. She'd turn around about 150 yards out and hang out treading water. I was in awe of how graceful she looked in the water. When she'd had enough, she'd swim back to shore.

While in Maui, we were snorkeling in front of the condo and she wanted to join in. Jon was showing her how to put the mask over her eyes and the snorkel in her mouth, while I held Riley at the shoreline. At first bite of the mouthpiece she was spitting it out and saying she didn't think she could do it because of the salty taste. Once she got past that and had the mask and snorkel on, the next step was to swim out, put her face in the water, and look below to see what the reef had to offer. She was not comfortable putting her face in the water and breathing through the snorkel. Her reaction was priceless. She jerked her whole body back in surprise. What a jolt! She had us all laughing. Needless to say, that was the end of snorkeling for her.

I am not sure how or when our goofy dressing room escapades started, but I know they began with Riley. Whenever I'd take him to try on clothes, he would become a full-on comedian in the dressing room. Our shopping excursions took extra-long due to the time we spent laughing and being joyful. I could not be in a hurry when it came to clothes shopping with the boys. I am sure the clerks wondered what in the world was going on behind the closed door. To this day, there is something that comes unleashed for the boys when they get in front of the mirror behind the door of a dressing room. They have the same sense of humor and know exactly what to do and say to start the contagious cackle crank in motion.

Humor can be a respite from sadness and pain. It can lighten your mood and even inspire hope. A laugh can bring your mind and body into balance. It's a cheap way to lighten your spirits. Since it is an instinctive behavior, all you need to do is set yourself up to be around people who are laughing, or put yourself in a situation where humor could evolve. You have little conscious control over laughter as it is spontaneous, so it could be a good antidote for the Debbie Downer behavior you may be exhibiting. When you're somber it can be difficult to believe anything can bring you joy. I encourage you to write a list of ideas where you have the potential to laugh and then try one on for size and see how it goes. You may be surprised by your own laughter. Here's a list I put together. Some you can do alone, and others involve "others." What's great about being with others is that you're more likely to laugh and it can strengthen your relationship bonds.

- Get together with friends/family
- Do a fun activity (e.g. dance, karaoke, bowling, video games)

- Take a class (e.g. painting, glassblowing, cooking, trapeze)
- Watch a funny movie, TV show (SNL is my favorite), or YouTube video
- Go to a comedy club, or watch stand up on TV
- Read or listen to a funny book
- Host or go to a game night
- Play with a pet or kids
- Do something silly (use Snapchat filters to distort your face)
- Stand in front of a carnival mirror (to distort your entire body)
- People watch at a park or café and make up silly stories about what you see
- Get out of your comfort zone and try something new (laugh at yourself in the process)

I have done all the above and can honestly say these are all things that have brought a smile to my face. About a year after my mom died, I listened to the audiobook *The Know-It-All: One Man's Humble Quest to Become the Smartest Person in the World*, read by the author, A.J. Jacobs. He was incredibly witty. I couldn't help but laugh out loud at him and the crazy information he shared from his quest to read the *Encyclopaedia Britannica* from A to Z. It was awesome! I like to have at least one audiobook on my phone that's comical. Life can get heavy at times and it helps lighten it up with a touch of a finger. I put my phone in my back pocket and go about my business, which could be folding clothes, making breakfast, or taking a walk.

I've also read about laughing, that we can make it part of our daily routine. Like our regular cup of coffee. While you're sipping your cup of joe, you could throw on a video of little kids dancing. *America's Funniest Home Videos* is a favorite pastime TV show that gets me laughing. The footage is raw and comes from viewers who had captured a cat falling in a bathtub, a son accidentally hitting his dad in the crotch with a bat, or maybe a baby trying a new food. All good, clean fun!

Laughing may do the following:

- Boost the immune system
- Lower blood pressure
- Create connection
- Burn calories
- Release endorphins
- Reduce stress
- Build your confidence
- Retain information
- Ab workout

On the first Christmas without my mom, Dylan asked if we were going to get a tree and decorate. It was hard for me to fathom finding any joy in the rituals and traditions we had been accustomed to. I put that aside for the sake of my sons and we decided to use my mom's fake tree for our Tannenbaum. We had a tradition of all going to pick out a live tree, so this was a big change. When we put the tree together in our living room, we found we were missing a large section of the tree. Oh my! It looked ridiculous. More like a Christmas bush. We were rolling on the floor at the sad sight of this plastic scrub. To me it was perfectly imperfect. My mom would have been bursting at the seams!

You can even have a good laugh while you're dreaming. When Dylan was six-and-a-half, I heard him laughing out loud after I had tucked him in, and it was clearly past his bedtime. I peeked into his room and he was asleep but laughing. Wow! It was entertaining to be a witness to my little boy finding humor in his sleep. It must have been quite an amusing dream.

More recently, I was attending an awards banquet for the 2019 NMA off-roading racing season. Dylan was receiving a first-place award for the Open A division. He is a mighty fast dirt bike rider! After the ceremony, I wanted to tell everyone a joke, but then couldn't remember it. Jon started teasing me because I'm famous for not being able to remember punch-lines. I was cracking up at myself, which had Dylan laughing at me and then his girlfriend Leila was probably laughing at the both of us. I looked the joke up on my phone as I remembered it was about an owl and a rooster. When I found the joke, I discovered it was dirtier than I remembered, which got me laughing and crying along with Dylan and Leila. The buildup was so much more amusing than the actual joke: "What do you get when you cross an owl with a rooster? A cock that stays up all night!"

There's nothing like laughing uncontrollably. You don't plan it, you don't know it is going to happen and, in the end, you are left feeling euphoric. Especially when you are laughing at yourself and with people you love. I encourage you to elicit your laughing lingo—snort, cackle, crow, giggle, sniggle, chortle, chuckle, guffaw, howl, shriek, snicker, snigger, titter, twitter, roar, crack up, burst out, get hysterical, be in stitches, lose it, cry tears of laughter, wet yourself, split your sides and experience fits of laughter. Even just reading all the words associated with laughing will raise your spirits! Har-de-har, tehee, ha-ha, lol.

CHAPTER 16:

Meaningful Memories

*"Sometimes you will never know the true value of
a moment until it becomes a memory."*
—Anonymous

Whenever I utter the word memory, I think of Barbara Streisand singing her Oscar winning song, "The Way We Were." This is from the 1973 romantic movie starring her and Robert Redford when opposites attract. This song may be from one lover to another, but the words hold truth to them for anyone reflecting on memories of a loved one gone. It has a distinctly sentimental value, but also a tinge of hope. The song ends with the line, "It is the laughter we will remember." Sage advice, and important to keep in mind as we make our way through the one life we're given.

When a loved one dies, all we have are the memories of them and the times we shared. It is a priceless gift. It was often hard for me to summon memories, knowing they'd make me sad, but ultimately they were my savior. Looking at photo albums, talking to family and friends, or conjuring my mom up in my mind, all brought me closer to her and the love we shared. My memories of her are my own and they will stay with me as long as I live.

In the beginning, I had plenty of conversations with others about my mom. It's what we do to heal: we share stories about those who have passed and how they related to us. These conversations lessened as time went on and admittedly this hurt. I wanted everyone to continue talking about her, keeping her alive, remembering and loving her as much as I did. This is impossible, however, because we are all individuals with grieving methods of our own. My approach was to see it all, feel it all, and share with anyone who would listen. I was afraid that if I didn't talk about her, my memories would wane, and my sons wouldn't remember her at all. I know now I don't recall everything, but I remember enough to bring a smile to my face and relish the momentous impact she had on my life.

Writing this book evoked memories of my mom that were hidden in my mind. It was a welcome respite for me to relive so many misplaced moments. I am fortunate to have journaled after she died, writing down stories that others shared and memories as they came to me. At differing times in my life I thought I'd recollect all of the things I experienced with my mom over the years, but I don't have an ironclad memory, so I tend to remember the extreme highs or the lowest of the lows. The everyday events, not so much. It is the habitual acts of mundane activity that make up our real life. The duty of our days demonstrates who we are. What we eat for breakfast, what we do for work, what books we read, what shows we watch, and who we spend time with. All of it envelops the essence of who we are and many of my memories of my mom are just that—ordinary occurrences of her life and the life she shared with me, Jon, Riley, and Dylan.

In the fall after her death, we were at Dave's house for a barbecue. He lit a fire in the fireplace, and I was standing in front of it to get warm, as I'm constantly seeking heat. While I was defrosting, I remembered how my mom would dance around in front of the fire making silly noises. We always had a fireplace in our houses, and I recalled her doing this animated act. She was tickled to be thawing out and would demonstrate her gratitude with this ritualistic hooting noise while waving her hands in front and behind her in a hand-jive type motion, making sure her tush was close to the fire for maximum toasting.

While I was in front of the fire, I told Dave about this memory and he said, "She always added a little fun to everything." He hit the bullseye with that remark. Everyone who knew her would be inclined to agree.

I grew up burping. Kooky to say, but true. Yes. I know we all burp, but mine were burly burps. Not ladylike ones. My mom, my Grandma Flo, and my Uncle Rick (my mom's brother) all had big burps. It's who I grew up around and what I grew up with. I was accustomed to belching loudly in my own home. Sometimes I'd close my mouth, and sometimes I'd belt it out. I must swallow an immense amount of air when I eat and drink to release such a cacophony. I'm not sure if this is a learned behavior or in my genes. My Grandma Flo told me with the utmost certainty it was a sign of a good meal when you'd burp afterwards. Her parents were descendants from England and Britain, and I thought maybe it came from her ancestors in Europe. Interestingly, burping is considered good manners and a sign of appreciation for the hospitality in Bahrain, China, and India. It makes me feel a little better to know that in some parts of the world it's a polite thing to do.

It had almost been a year since my mom passed when Jon, the boys, and I were talking at the dinner table one night. I must have belted one out and then in short order told them of my ancestral burping history. I found it important to tell them anything that reminded me of my mom, especially if it was a family trait. Jon was not a fan of my burping. In fact, I am not sure if he burps at all. We were together for twenty-eight years and I can't remember any air escaping his mouth. Regardless of this fact, I wanted to share with my sons about their relatives, even if it wasn't the most glowing attribute. I am of the belief that when you speak of a loved one and share their stories, you can create new memories of them with each other.

The boys are young men now and seem to have gotten used to their mom being able to scare young children with a single belch. I don't do it in public, so at least I am not embarrassing them with this bodily function. I can't say I don't embarrass them in other ways. I am their mom, after all. When I burp today, Dylan will say, "Lori Belcher," as if to say, "There she goes again." My mom would find his nickname for me a fitting choice. Nonetheless, burps are a fond memory I have of my mom and a trait that has been passed down generation to generation. It pleases me to say that I believe she'd be proud.

It's interesting to me how a memory will come to you when you are doing something similar to what you remember your loved one doing. I was mowing our lawn the spring after my mom died; outfitted in shorts and a tank top, when memories of my mom came flooding in. I could see her in her denim cutoff jeans, tank top, and tennis shoes mowing my childhood lawn. We had a white electric lawn mower with a twisted orange extension cord. She'd go up and down the yard mowing the lawn, tugging at the cord. I remember her telling me she enjoyed mowing the lawn. At the time I couldn't pinpoint why, until I had my own lawn to mow. There's something about being outside, seeing the fruits of your labor and smelling fresh cut grass. When you are done, not only is the grass shorter, but it looks so much better and you have a sense of accomplishment. That day and all the times I've mowed the lawn since I feel closer to her.

Growing up, my mom was not a good cook. She told me her mom was not a very good cook and that was passed down. Apparently, the English are not known for their culinary creations. They are known to cook bland meals. I can confirm this to be true based on my visit to England in 2017. I didn't find the local food to be flavorful. My mom would often overcook or burn food. Gobs of gray and charred steak appeared on my dinner plates. It was a running joke that she'd get distracted or have one too many cocktails and forget she was making dinner. I think her less-than-stellar culinary skills had more to do with not having much money to buy certain ingredients, and also her limited time as a single hardworking mom, to be creative.

When I was an adult, she became a wonderful cook. She enjoyed the process of growing her own vegetables, canning tomato sauce for pasta, and making her own salsa. She took pride in the food she made, and you could taste it in the flavors. Some of my fondest food memories from childhood are desserts she'd make. Peanut butter cookies were easy, and we usually had all the ingredients for them around the house. I have the recipe for these cookies she wrote out in her own handwriting.

Every time I use it, I think of her whipping up a batch in our yellow-walled kitchen with green curtains.

The second Christmas we spent without her, we were at Jon's sister's house for a tree-trimming party. Coral served us a delicious dessert of gingerbread cake with a dollop of whipped cream on the top. This was a Christmastime staple when I was growing up. No recipe required. Just a box of gingerbread cake mix and whipped cream, or Cool Whip. Easy peasy! The smell that would fill the house, with its gingery aroma coupled with the fir tree scent, was unmistakably Christmas. The finished moist cake was a palate pleaser, striking the perfect balance of spongy and firm. The whipped topping was a light and refreshing addition to each individual bite. All in all, this dessert is not too rich in taste or on the pocketbook.

I don't have one grandiose occasion to encapsulate my relationship with my mom or our life together. What I have are thirty-seven years of being in a mother-daughter relationship, sharing our dreams, accomplishments, failures, desires, sadness, and all the simple and absolutely wonderful pleasures in life. I am a fortunate daughter to have had all this time with my mom. I would love to have more, but I am at peace with what is. I can call upon my memories when I want to see her, hear her, and feel her. She is never far, as I carry her in my heart.

CHAPTER 17:

Honoring Her Memory

"When those you love die, the best you can do is honor
their spirit for as long as you live. You make a commitment
that you're going to take whatever lesson that person or
animal was trying to teach you, and you make it true in
your own life . . . It's a positive way to keep their spirit alive
in the world, by keeping it alive in yourself."
—Patrick Swayze

By age thirty-seven, I hadn't been to many memorials, but knew
I wanted to honor my mom in a way she would have enjoyed.
I was all too familiar with grief, having been born five months
after my dad died. My mom carried me in her womb at eighteen,
knowing she was bringing her daughter into the world fatherless
and that already at such a young age she was a widow. I believe I
was born with a cellular sadness passed along to me by my mom's
grief while I was growing in her belly. As a little girl I ached for

my dad and would pray for him to come back to me. At some point, I understood this was never going to happen.

My mom never remarried, so I didn't have any father figures among the men she dated. I did have my Uncle Rick, though. He was kind, smart, funny, athletic, a role model, and never forgot my birthday. He was the closest man in my life to a dad, and then he died when I was thirteen. All I remember of his memorial was sobbing uncontrollably at the church. I wasn't old enough to comprehend how to grieve and there wasn't anyone to help me along.

Since my Grandma Flo hadn't wanted a memorial and my mom honored that wish, the Celebration of Life we planned for my mom became a way for me to honor and grieve my dad, my uncle, and my grandma. I was now an adult orphan grieving all the losses of my first family. I had the tools of an adult and could honor and grieve them in a way that resonated with me. After all, memorials are for the living—those of us who desire the connection of our loved one to still be intact. We come together to talk about them, tell stories, laugh, cry, and share a meal—all to have a common bond with another human being who is grieving the same loss. Honoring her memory was a testament to how much I loved her and how deeply saddened I was that she was gone. More important, the acts, events, and ways I honored her were opportunities for me to heal.

Jon and I hosted the Celebration of Life a few weeks after my mom passed. We chose a local venue right on the water where you could watch boats passing by as they entered and exited the Ballard Locks. It was such a picturesque backdrop. She would have been delighted with the vibe of this setting. I also know she would have loved and appreciated the attention to detail we put into the day to make it all about her. It was important to me to emanate her aura. We chose food she loved, music she'd groove to, photographs she'd laugh at, flowers she'd adore, and spoken words she'd be grateful to hear. It was a group effort to coordinate all of this so quickly and I am grateful for all the friends and family who lent their time and skills to make it a joyous occasion celebrating Kathy Lynn Cook.

My mom spent a lot of her youth at Lake Chelan with her family, and I spent many summers there with her. I have such warm memories of times spent with her, my Grandma Flo, and Uncle Rick, lounging on air mattresses and picnicking in the grass. Deviled eggs made by my grandma were a favorite staple, peppered with plenteous paprika. A beach bum's beloved bite-sized bounty. It was a favorite place to be in the sun and go for a dip in the cold, clean, and refreshing water. My mom wanted to be cremated and she told Dave her desire was to be buried next to my dad in Wenatchee. She had never told me this, so I am grateful she expressed this wish to him. She loved this lake and being outside, so I decided to put some of her ashes in the lake and the rest next to my dad. Two months after she passed, Dave, Jon, the boys, and I went to Lake Chelan and stayed in a condo together. We rented a boat, got flung around in the innertube, swam, and felt closer to her doing all these activities she loved. A little of her still swims in the lake and I know she's smiling.

I created three scrapbooks, which included cards, letters, photos, newspaper articles, and safe driving efforts I was championing. I made a page for each person who gave us a condolence card and added photos of the person, or my mom with them. We asked guests at the Celebration of Life to write something about my mom—a memory, a thought, or how they knew her. I added those to the scrapbook, too. It amazed me how many people saw my mom as I did, as a kindhearted woman with a wonderful smile who was full of laughter. She was a compassionate presence in others' lives.

The scrapbooks were another way to honor her, her benevolent soul and what she meant to others. I'd sit and read the cards and I would weep and weep.

I recently pulled the scrapbooks out of the hope chest to jog my memory and I am grateful I took the time and energy to leave a trace of my mom. That's how I feel, too, about writing this book. My sons can look through these pages later on and see how many lives she touched and what kind of person she was in the world. They will have the story of who my mother was and how she informed me. I am glad they have that, and I am happy to be capturing the multifaceted woman she was so that her memory can live on.

I found a sympathetic condolence card from a stranger at the crash site. It was a confirmation of how we are all linked, and one life has a ripple on countless others, even if they never knew one another. Here is what it said:

"Don't know who you were. I know where you are. I'm not religious just spiritual. It would be great to be you. I drive the route 522 often. Don't know if you are a bus rider or not. If so, I don't know if you just got off of a bus or were going to get on a bus. I'm wearing sunglasses today. It is sunny & beautiful. And my eyes are welling up. I thought this balloon would be appropriate. Butterflies. Free, beautiful, and moving unlike any other winged species. Light & unassuming. They will land on a total stranger's shoulder. A peaceful creature. Calm, full of faith. I don't know you. But I feel you inside me. Thank you for giving me tears."

This card and the dozens of eyewitness statements I read about the crash gave me the idea to create a memorial garden at the crash site. My mom died on a busy highway on a sunshiny day in June. Many people witnessed her death and reading their statements was devastating. The statements came from bus riders, people in their cars at the intersection, employees working at nearby businesses, and the other pedestrians who were hit. She had a very public and tragic death. I couldn't imagine what kind of indelible impact witnessing that tragedy might have on a person. I had a hard time deciding if a memorial garden at the site would be a gruesome reminder of her death, or a lovely testament to her life. I wanted to change the spot from a place of death to a place of life. She was a gifted gardener, so planting a tree and flowers would have been a true tribute to her spirit.

I contacted the City of Kenmore about the possibility of the memorial garden and they were not only all for it, they contributed financially to its formation. Around that time, Riley had a sixth-grade community service project to complete and this became his charter. It also turned into a family activity where we could all participate. Riley, Dylan, and I started out by visiting a rock center and choosing a rugged-looking boulder that made the perfect sitting bench and a smooth surfaced rock to display a bronze memorial plaque. Our next stop was Bedrock Industries. I love this place and go there often for artistic inspiration. The bevy of colored mosaic glass cullet and the troupe of tumbled glass shapes awakens something inside me to create, like the awe I observe when witnessing the vivid colors of an ephemeral rainbow. On our trip we gathered a gallimaufry of glass for our steppingstones.

Jon, Riley, Dylan, and I each made a steppingstone for our yard and some for the memorial garden. We constructed a large square together with our names, handprints, and individually chosen glass pieces. When everything was complete, we planted an assortment of my mom's favorite flowers, and the city planted a Witch Hazel tree at my request. It blooms a light, sweet flowery fragrance with small yellow petals in December. It's a lovely reminder of beauty in the darkness of winter. I chose this tree because we have a large older one in our backyard and my mom loved it, as do I. When it is blossoming, I go outside and inhale a large whiff through my sniffing nose. It's like I'm smelling a succulent piece of tropical ripe fruit. The bouquet is brief, so when I spy the tawny leaves on the mossy backdrop of the branches I rush for the aroma.

When the memorial garden was complete, I phoned and invited all the crash survivors and our family and friends to meet for a gathering. Only one survivor attended, but there were plenty of family and friends. It happened to be raining that day in August 2008, which seemed appropriate for a new beginning. A cleansing with water for new life.

Over the years I've gone to the garden with my boys, and with family and friends, often to do a spring and fall clean-up or new plantings. Just like life, the garden is evolving. To this day, passersby will ask me what happened, or tell me they were there that day. We chat for a spell and oftentimes people comment on how much they appreciate the remembrance. Since the crash, the grieving and healing I experienced brought me in closer connection with all people and all creatures of the earth. We are all connected to each other. When you experience this awareness, you have an immense amount of compassion. I am easier going and less judgmental of others than I was. I can see myself in others and understand that we all are at different stages in our journey. The most enlightened among us will demonstrate deep wisdom, insight, and open-mindedness. The less enlightened will show fear, ignorance, and intolerance. Understanding this reasoning can help you let go of how you believe situations and people should be and accept them as they are.

A more traditional marker of honoring one's life is a headstone and graveside memorial. When Dave told me my mom wanted to be buried next to my dad in Wenatchee where she and I were both born, I thought it to be an ideal arrangement. Dave generously offered to pay for the headstone, and we worked together to create a visual we both agreed embodied her. Etched into the pink stone, she is standing holding her dog Holly with passion flowers at her feet on one side and a stalk of dahlias and a frog on a lily pad on the other. It's so her! My Wenatchee family, my grandpa and his wife from Spokane, along with Dave, his dad, Jon, me, and the boys, had a service together where we buried her ashes. She rests next to her first love, my dad, Larry Gene Cook. I am grateful I have this place to visit my parents and Dave's graciousness in honoring my mom's wishes. It also leaves a trace they were here and loved.

A less conventional but a favorite way in which I honor my mom is to spend time doing things that remind me of her. In the summer I will don my bikini, put a lawn chair out in the yard, and prop myself up for some sun time. I might even paint my toenails while I'm out there. She had a thing about painting her toenails while she was sitting in the sun. I've followed in her footsteps. She had the cutest size 5.5 feet, the daintiest toenails and stood at five-foot-five. I can't say the same for my feet and toes. She called them gunboats. They are a whopping size 8.5 and pushing a 9 and I am only one inch taller than her. While I am sunbathing, I will be accompanied by the sounds of the Doobie Brothers, Van Morrison, or maybe some Tom Petty tunes. And always with some nibbles to gnaw on while I soak up vitamin D and retreat into a sun-induced nap. She'd love this!

Her DNA and imprint live on in me as we have similar traits. Every day my mannerisms, laugh, silly voices, and sayings honor her and what we shared. She had a comically crass saying when she got frustrated or mad and I say it too: "Fuck a duck!" she'd exclaim. Every time I say it, I giggle and think of her. She is part of me, part of my sons, and will live on in their children if they have them. She loved being a grandma and I can see why. You are older, wiser, and more patient once your own kids are grown. I look forward to the time when I am a grandma.

My mom kept her original wedding ring intact and tucked away in her jewelry box. As a little girl I'd admire it and wonder what she'd look like wearing it and being a wife. When my Grandma Flo died, my grandpa gave my mom her wedding ring. I was surprised he had kept it for forty years, but extremely grateful. When we were visiting him once, he told the story of buying the diamond during World War II. He was stationed in North Africa and bought it there. Not from a jewelry store, but off someone who sold him a diamond necklace.

He met my grandma after the war as they both worked at the Brecksville Veterans Administration Hospital in Ohio. He was from Ohio and she was originally from Canada, but had been living in Wenatchee before she enlisted into the Women's Army Corps. I had both of their rings and knew I wanted to combine the two diamonds to make a piece of jewelry honoring them. It would be an ensemble I could wear to be reminded of the two women who loved and supported me the most. I don't wear much jewelry, so it took me a while to decide what to do. I ended up getting a necklace custom-made. It is a delicate gold chain in a princess-style length, ending at the top of my breastbone. My grandma's diamond, the larger of the two, is the focal point, and my mom's diamond drops down from it. They are joined. It's my favorite piece of jewelry and when I wear it I feel a sense of support, pride, and heritage.

These are a few examples of how I chose to honor my mom's memory. I continue to honor her as it has become part of who I am. I still miss her presence in my life, but can reflect upon the times we were together, support she provided, and love we shared to get me through my sadness. I am grateful for the time we had with one another and our close relationship. When she was killed, she was stolen from me and I was fucking angry. I wanted more time with her. More time for the boys with their grandma. More time for HER to live HER life. I now understand how important it is to appreciate those in your life because all we have is the present moment. The ones you love today may not be here tomorrow. Life is amazing but very fragile. Treat it with loving kindness. Treat yourself and others with loving kindness.

CHAPTER 18:

Gratitude

*"The greatest thing is to give thanks for
everything. He who has learned this knows what
it means to live. He has penetrated the whole
mystery of life: giving thanks for everything."*
—ALBERT SCHWEITZER

A few months after my mom died, I saw the author Elizabeth
Gilbert on *The Oprah Show*. She suggested writing down your
happiest moment at the end of each day. This can help you
to be aware of what you have in your life to be grateful for.
I started doing it that very night and was surprised by what
made me happy. It was everyday occurrences that were seem-
ingly banal but also breathtakingly beautiful. I was alive, and
the people and pets I loved were, too. I found more joy every
day when I looked for the happy moments. Being devastated
by such a tremendous loss can overtake your life with grief,

depression, and cynicism. It is hard to see the light when you are surrounded by your own veil of darkness. This simple daily task helped me comprehend what I had in my life to be grateful for. Here are some of the nuggets I unearthed.

On the first day, one of my happiest moments was watching Etta and Holly play tug-of-war with Etta's leash. Whenever I'd gear them up for a walk, I'd put on Etta's leash and she'd pick it up and carry it in her mouth. Then she'd shoot out the front door as fast as she could. Holly was an instigator of trouble, so she'd chase after Etta, grab her leash, and immediately start pulling on it and start growling. Etta would pull back and prance around the yard while Holly was seriously hell-bent to get the leash from her.

The tugging and pulling commenced. Etta had about forty pounds on Holly, so it was comical to watch this push and pull Lindy Hop-type dance between two determined dogs. Etta was such a sweet soul and seemed to get a kick out of Holly's dogged diligence. At some point I'd call to Etta to stop and she'd drop her part of the leash and we'd be off on our walk. Holly would still be amped up and try to get the leash, but eventually she would calm down as the walk went on.

Two other moments I noted were reading a book in the living room and tucking in my sons. Bedtime with my boys was like our nighttime networking—a time to talk, cuddle, and take away the day's stress. To leave it all behind to recuperate and rejuvenate with a good night's sleep. This was a nightly routine I did without much thought, but I became conscious of how much these daily occurrences brought me beatitude.

When I looked back at my journal for these happy moments, I saw they were mostly categorized into three buckets: my relationships with others, nature, and music.

On relationships with others, one notable moment happened during a regular exchange at the mailboxes. My neighbor Leauri and I were talking about something and laughing. She has such an infectious laugh it made me laugh even more. I could see in this moment how important my relationships were with other people. All people. I love seeing others happy. My empathy reminded me that everyone suffers and anyone who can embody happiness brings me an immense amount of joy, because I know by nature everyone's life is vulnerable to pain and suffering.

On nature, I wake up grateful every day to live in a comfortable home and in a neighborhood surrounded by evergreen trees, snow-capped mountains, the Puget Sound, and stunning sunsets. When I walk out my front door I can hear the ferry's low mournful wail of a foghorn reverberating through the misty air, or the whistle of the train as it rumbles along the tracks. These are the harmonies of my hood. The natural notes I am grateful for burst from the birds: the electric buzz of the hummingbirds and their fast beating wings, the caw of the crows, the nighttime hooting of the Barred owls, and the singing of the chickadees, robins and spotted towhees. There are times I am overwhelmed by the avian opera emitted from my backyard. My absolute favorite time is when they are all feeding, trilling, and singing together. I am amazed how all these birds came to my backyard to eat at the exact same moment. They don't seem to mind each other at all and go about their business foraging for food. I crack a window or go out on my deck to get a better bite of the sound. It was all so surreal. A mysterious menagerie of my own feathered friends feasting feverishly.

On music, whether it be my family jamming out in the rec room, music piped through the grocery store, or a concert

I attended, I often find myself smiling and being groovy-tunes grateful for music. I love how music gets me out of my thoughts and into my body. It takes over and my human vessel wants to swing and sway. Even if it is just a toe tap. It's so natural. You can see it in children. They have no inhibitions. They just move to the music any way it strikes them. It's perfect.

The summer after my mom passed, Jon and I took the boys to a concert at the zoo where Shawn Mullins and the Avett Brothers were performing. Kids were running around, chasing each other, rolling down hills, and dancing. They were so in their bodies. I enjoyed being out in the world to relish in their exuberance and glee. Their energy was contagious. I was a mirror reflecting their vivacious vitality back to me. I was alive and blissful.

It's easy to wander to the dark side and complain about the pettiest shit. So it's important to reel ourselves back in and see the reality of our situations. These remembrances all help me to think about the fact that I'm alive and have the where-withal to make choices in how I think and act. Life is too short to be mired down in worry, complaints, and pessimism. Find what simple pleasures in life bring you joy, balance, and grati-tude. Like connecting with others, getting outside, or turning on some music to boogie. Once you open this can of worms you may be surprised at what squirms out. I love anything soft and warm. My socks, my robe, blankets, my pillow, the top of Etta's silky soft head and her plush petable ears. I am open to what may come. I set aside my expectations, as those tend to lead to disappointment. When I leave situations, or rather my mind open, I am pleasantly delighted by what shows up.

CHAPTER 19:

Safe Driving Saves Lives

"Sometimes, you have to get angry to get things done."
—ANG LEE

Becoming a midlife orphan at thirty-seven was a life-altering event. It was loss so deep, like a meteor lacerating a Grand Canyon-sized crater in my heart. The initial news of her death was unbelievable to me. How could she be dead? I had just spoken to her that morning and was waiting for her to come over that evening. It had to be a mistake. There was no way she could have been hit by a truck. Life could not be that cruel to me. To have three out of four people from my first family die in auto-related crashes was just too much to take in. No fucking way.

My disbelief was soon supported by the facts. Then came the utter bombshell to my system. The shutdown of my mind and an out of body fog-induced numbness came over me. I was disconnected from myself as if I were in a dream. I was watching myself from the periphery, on the outer edges of my own existence. It started with a call from a medical examiner asking me if I had seen the news about a crash on Bothell Way. I knew instantly the only reason a medical examiner calls is to tell you someone has died. I sensed it was my mom before he could get the words out. I had tried to reach her several times; she was supposed to be at our house and hadn't yet arrived, which was very unlike her.

He proceeded to tell me how she died, and that he didn't think she'd felt any pain as the injuries were severe and it was most likely instantaneous. I don't remember much else after that. My solid foothold in life was annihilated in a single phone call. All I had known to be stable, secure, and grounding disintegrated in an instant, and I could not fix it. Death is permanent, final, an absolute end. I was falling deeper and deeper into a void of nothingness as my family floor collapsed underneath me. My mind spiraled into a black abyss of disbelief. I was a shell of a person going through the motions of what needed to get done. I had two children to take care of and I needed to remain sane. If it weren't for them, I am not sure how I would have survived this loss. I had some desperately low times where I didn't want to keep living. The agony was soul searing. I couldn't imagine in those moments it would ever subside. I was exhausted by myself and my incessant brooding over the morbid details of her death and the senseless way she died. It was unimaginable to me someone could run a red light eight seconds after it was red. As the only casualty, I couldn't help but think, *Why her? Why couldn't it have been someone else?* I hated myself for having such thoughts, but I did. I'd had enough loss in my life. It was grossly unfair.

After the crash, I was vulnerable when it came to anything auto-related. I was scared to be on the road with all the distracted and unsafe drivers. I became a vigilantly defensive driver. I was constantly on the lookout for others turning in front of me, stopping too quickly, weaving in and out of their lanes, and I exercised extraordinary trepidation traveling through intersections with potential red light runners. I also feared people close to me were going to die in crashes. I know now I had post-traumatic stress. But a pervasive thought ran through my mind: *Was my family cursed, unlucky, or were we all destined to die this way?* When friends and family heard the news, they would comment that it was unbelievable that this could have happened to me again, and how sorry they were. It was less like sympathy and more like they felt sorry for me. I didn't want their pity. In hindsight, I don't think their intention was to feel sorry for me; but this was how I felt about my situation. I felt sorry for myself.

It is human nature to desire to understand the who, what, where, when, why, and how of a situation. I was no different when it came to the crash. I thought the details would help me make sense of a senseless situation. I had several conversations over the first few months with the detective on the case. He was kind, but also very direct in telling me to educate myself on the vehicular homicide laws in Washington state. What I found is that you have to be drunk, on drugs, or driving with a blatant disregard for the safety of others to be convicted, or have any sort of repercussions.

In my mom's case, it wasn't clear what the driver was or wasn't doing that distracted him to drive through a red light at full speed. He could have been on his phone, but he claimed he wasn't. A witness said they saw the driver moving his hands like he was in a conversation with someone, but no one else was in the truck. Unfortunately, the police didn't summon the phone records of the phone soon enough. Apparently, the cell phone company didn't keep records longer than thirty days, and I'll never know what circumstances led up to them not making this request in a timely way. In my mind, the driver exhibited a conscious disregard for the safety of others, but the prosecutor didn't charge him with anything.

The injustice of this reality hit me like a ton of bricks. I spoke to the victim's advocate from the prosecuting attorney's office. We spent an hour and a half on the phone, she explaining to me why the driver was not being charged with vehicular homicide. He would only receive a ticket in the amount of $250 for second-degree negligent driving. It was incomprehensible to me he could kill my mom and injure six other people and receive such a minimal fine. Laws punish drivers who are under the influence of alcohol or drugs, or who show a blatant disregard for the safety of others. He was not under the influence and even though he ran a red light eight seconds after it was red, it was not enough to prove he had a blatant disregard for the safety of others. If others had seen him weaving in and out of lanes or driving erratically for miles, he could have been charged. Even crazier, he could defer paying at all if he hadn't had a previous ticket in the last seven years. My blood boiled with anger. How could this be? A person can make such an egregious mistake and not have any repercussions from it? It was not an accident, as it could have been avoided. He was clearly not paying attention. All the witnesses say his light was red when he claimed it was green.

My anger motivated me to focus my efforts on safe driving advocacy. I was determined to make a difference in the world to honor my mom, dad, and uncle's lives. Within a few months of my mom's death, I read a book called *It's No Accident: The Real Story Behind Senseless Death and Injury on Our Roads,* written by Lisa Lewis. I was surprised to learn that car crashes were the biggest killer in the U.S. for people ages four to thirty-four and the biggest cause of brain injuries.

She shone a light on the death and destruction on our roadways to raise awareness about safe driving efforts, current laws, and the time and economic impact on Americans from avoidable crashes. I reached out to her and we talked on the phone about her crash-prevention campaign. I found it interesting she had never had a family member die in a crash but was so passionate about the subject. She was talking to the United States Senate about a safe driving proposal at the time of our conversation. I wanted to make a difference and asked how I could help. I made calls to the Senate, donated to the partnership by getting their logo refreshed and had bumper stickers made with the message "Safe Driving Saves Lives." I sent an email to everyone I knew with the subject line: Sharing My Story. I told them of my family history and how my mom was killed by a distracted driver. My request was for them to think about their own driving habits. I encouraged everyone I communicated with to drive safely.

I followed up when the bumper stickers were ready. I was happy that a number of folks wanted to put a sticker on their car. I had an interesting comment from a friend and could completely appreciate what she was saying. She said, "I feel a tremendous responsibility to drive safe with this sticker on my car."

My response, "Wouldn't it be great if everyone felt that way when driving, sticker or no sticker?"

I had some fears about focusing my attention on safe driving efforts. Would people listen? Would they see me as a vigilante? Would I be taking time away from my family? All these questions crossed my mind and I grappled with them for two years while devoting my time and energy trying to make an impact. I can see now that what is important to me is not important to everyone else. I am the main character in the play of my life, so what I deem to be imperative is generally not the case for another. They have their own life experiences, which lead them to regard what is significant for their well-being.

At the time I couldn't grasp how someone could not perceive this to be one of the highest-priority problems in our community. In 2007, I could see we had become an instant-gratification society with technology, and especially with our cell phones. By the writing of this book in 2020, it's only gotten worse. The expectation is that you will pick up and answer a call or respond to a text immediately. Since everyone always has their phone with them, it is anticipated they will choose to respond right away. The reality is—we have a choice. I remember the days of letters and answering machines. You knew you had to wait for a response, as it was the norm. Frankly, I wish we would allow more leniency for that choice. People have other stuff going on and the world doesn't revolve around us and our selfish needs.

My initial safe driving advocacy goals were lofty. I wanted to create a new law, a law with teeth behind it, one with repercussions for drivers who killed or injured another by crashing their 3,000-pound weapon into another human being. From my perspective, the existing laws were atrociously inadequate. I saw this as a big loophole in the justice system. If you wanted to kill someone and get away with it, just do it with your car. I know this oversimplifies everything, but it seemed straightforward to me. You could receive a stiffer penalty for littering in some states or driving solo in the carpool lane, a flagrantly immoral flaw.

Meanwhile, I investigated making the streets safer in my own neighborhood. Specifically, the main road the children in my community used to walk to school, catch the bus, and ride their bikes. The idea came to me while Dylan and I were riding our bikes. We were crossing the street and a car came speeding through with no regard for us or the speed limit. We both got a scare out of it. We went home and added some words to the back of the kids' lemonade stand sign they used in the summer. It read: "25 mph. Thank you." The boys and I stood on the corner with the sign and smiled and waved as drivers passed by, hoping to get them to look at their speed, recognize kids were around, and raise their awareness to drive safely.

There was another incident across the street from the boys' bus stop when a teenager came around the corner too fast, lost control, and took out a fence. To think there could have been a group of kids standing there instead of a fence was alarming. I talked to other parents and they agreed it felt unsafe with drivers speeding where our kids were walking and waiting. The speed limit on this arterial was twenty-five miles per hour, but people tended to go over thirty. I knew from my research that injuries to pedestrians increase significantly as the miles per hour go up. For example, if someone is hit by a car at twenty miles per hour, they are ten percent more likely to be killed versus fifty percent at thirty miles per hour. If I could raise awareness about the speed limit being twenty-five miles per hour, it could keep our kids and community a fraction safer.

I trotted down to my local police station to explain my concerns. They told me about their Neighborhood Traffic Safety Program, where community members can express issues they believe need to be addressed. The topics are evaluated by the city and something may or may not change because of it. I was happy to see my town had a program like this and I was onboard with trying to make a difference.

To kick off the operation, I had to find seven neighbors to sign a petition saying they agreed drivers were speeding on our road. It wasn't hard, as we had ten kids ages four to fourteen on our cul-de-sac alone. The end goal was to raise awareness of the speed limit and get drivers to slow down. Once the city reviewed the proposal and considered it worthy of further investigation, the process started in motion. The neighbors and I bought two KidAlert safety signs we named "Slow Steve" for our cul-de-sac. These were to remind drivers coming into our hood to SLOW DOWN. They were vibrant neon yellow and resembled a small kid wearing a ballcap holding an orange flag. At any time, there could be kids riding their bikes, playing tag, shooting hoops, or driving remote-controlled trucks around. Their safety was of the utmost importance.

The first step the City of Shoreline took was to place a pneumatic road tube sensor across the road. This counted how many vehicles traveled on the street each day. Four months later, they set up speed radar trailers to show drivers how fast they were going. A few months after that, they asked me to use a radar gun and record the speed at which vehicles were traveling on the road. Dylan and I stood on the sidewalk at different times of the day collecting data, mainly during times kids would be getting on and off the bus. I wondered if people were curious what a mom and her seven-year-old son were doing with a radar gun. An older couple we'd see walking every morning with coffees in hand, commented, "This is a good thing you are doing." Dylan and I took those words to heart.

About a week after our radar gun data collection, the city put radar trailers out again. I had done my job and they had done theirs. Now it was a waiting game to find out what conclusions they had come to. Three years after I started the process, the city painted 25 MPH in large white numbers and letters on the pavement in two spots within a five-block distance on the eight block road. It's hard to know if my goal was met or not, but I was satisfied something came out of the time and attention spent on the cause. Of course, I hope drivers will see the 25 MPH and that it will remind them to slow down and drive safely.

While I was partaking in the Neighborhood Traffic Safety Program, I was simultaneously looking into national, state, and local traffic safety laws and meeting with influencers. One of my first meetings was with the Washington Traffic Safety Commission. They are the state's designated highway safety office with a vision to reduce traffic fatalities and serious injuries on our roads. The gentlemen I met with offered to introduce me to anyone, but explained to me they were very political and focused on education campaigns, not new laws. As a newbie to the world of traffic safety and enacting of new laws I was deflated and disheartened by this response. I had no clue what steps to take, or who I should be introduced to. There was part of me wishing someone was as passionate as me about a new law and could sponsor it and help me navigate the system.

When I met with the prosecuting attorney I expressed wanting a law that would have repercussions for drivers who weren't under the influence who killed or injured others, or who were shown to have a blatant disregard for the safety of others. Possibilities could include jail time, hefty fines, attending safe driving school, restitution to victims, suspending/revoking licenses, or attending grief counseling/support groups with victims and their loved ones. We talked about Maria's Law and how it came about.

In 2004, a large piece of particle board broke free from an unsecured load, crashed through Maria Federici's windshield, and into her face, causing serious brain trauma, structural damage, and permanently taking away her sight. In the aftermath, Maria's mother, Robin Abel, went on a crusade to enact a law regarding unsecured loads. In 2005, Washington lawmakers passed "Maria's Law," criminalizing failure to properly secure a load. The prosecuting attorney told me this law had the support of the Seattle Police Department and she gave me the name of the then Seattle City Attorney who may be able to help me. It was in times like those I questioned my motives and how I was spending my time. Getting a new law enacted would take years. I wanted to make a difference on a grand scale, and this might have been clouding my judgment of what was right in front of me, my family that was alive. I wasn't ready to give up at this time, so I met with the Seattle City Attorney.

In my meeting with the Seattle City Attorney, he explained how there was a Seattle law in effect similar to the one I'd like to pass for a state law. It carried a penalty of one year of jail time and up to a $5,000 fine. I was full of questions about how there could only be a Seattle law and not a Washington State law like this. A Seattle council member's stepson had been hit as a pedestrian and incurred major injuries, including brain damage. He was able to use his position and leverage to navigate the system. It sure helps to be in the right place at the right time and know the right people. The Seattle City Attorney offered to support me in my quest for a state law.

I reached out to the mother of the boy who had been hit and discovered that she was a safe driving advocate as well. Andrea and I shared our stories and our common interest in stiffer laws, penalties, and safe driving education. She was interested in working with me on a state law. At this point I had several people who said they would support my efforts, but it was an overwhelming thing to tackle, especially given the undetermined outcome. I could put years of my life toward a new law and nothing may happen. I wasn't sure I was willing to give my time to this with all of the other priorities in my life—my marriage, my kids, my pets, my job, and my friends. How could I do it all and do any of it well?

Andrea suggested I talk to Robert Jamieson at the *Seattle Post-Intelligencer* to get some press around my mom's story. He wrote a social justice column and she was familiar with him due to her pedestrian safety efforts surrounding her son. I reached out and we ended up talking for three hours. He wanted to tell my family's story and get the word out. He sent a photographer to my house who took photos of me, the boys, and the dogs with the steppingstones, the photo boards of my mom, and the memorial scrapbooks. His article came out July 9, 2008. His writing style packed a punch of emotion and he wrote it like he knew my mom personally. I was proud of his story and his call to raise awareness about the dangers of distracted driving. A month later he published a second article about the memorial garden at the crash site. He wrote how a public tragedy like my mom's has a ripple effect on people's lives. I appreciated having someone other than my family or friends be as passionate about the cause as I was. Especially someone who had a voice in the community. He called attention to the poem on the memorial plaque: "Be present, be aware . . ." as offering advice for safe driving and for life.

I wasn't done trying to get support for a new law quite yet. In the summer of 2008, I spoke to Ruth Kagi, my Congresswoman at the time. I also phoned U.S. Senator Patty Murray's office for support. I met with Ruth in person and she offered her assistance but wasn't big on passing laws with penalties. She agreed to help me with awareness and education.

I spoke to the northwest region of the National Highway Traffic Safety Administration (NHTSA). They are an agency of the U.S. Federal Government, part of the Department of Transportation. Their mission is to "save lives, prevent injuries, reduce vehicle-related crashes." From my conversation I gleaned they were putting their money into seatbelt, drunk driving, and speed education because they had data and it was proven to work. They weren't focusing on distracted driving. There's a Federal Transportation bill every six years and states follow what the Feds say to focus on. You know why? Because that's what the Fed pays for.

I did discover that Washington is more progressive than most states. They had just passed a law where you would be fined if you were holding your cell phone in the car while talking on it. Six months later Washington had one for no texting and driving. Today twenty states, including D.C., Puerto Rico, Guam, and the U.S. Virgin Islands, prohibit all drivers from using hand-held cellphones while driving. And 48 states, D.C., Puerto Rico, Guam, and the U.S. Virgin Islands ban text messaging for all drivers. In the last thirteen years distracted driving due to cell phone use has become more prevalent. You can see the data included in NHTSA's traffic safety facts, including distracted driving in fatal crashes and driver electronic device use.

A friend of my Grandma Flo's sent me an article from the *Ladies Home Journal* about a law in Arizona she thought I'd be interested in. It was advocated for by a father named Frank Hinds after his teenage daughter was killed by a red light runner. It is called Jennifer's Law, fittingly named after his daughter. The law made it a punishable crime if you ran a red light and killed or maimed someone. The penalties are up to a $1,000 fine, your license suspended, and up to $10,000 in restitution to the family, community service, and sometimes jail time. Frank and two other parents affected by red light runners formed the Red Means Stop Traffic Safety Alliance in Arizona. Their long-term goal is to have the message about the dangers and consequences of red light running spread throughout the country until it is significantly reduced everywhere. After reading Frank's story and talking with him, I wondered if my scope was too broad. Maybe if I narrowed my focus to red light running I would have been more successful.

Frank asked if I'd speak at Mount Vernon High School, a school located fifty miles north of me, to tell my story. A student at the school was doing a public relations campaign around "Red Means Stop" for his senior project. He planned to include a mock car crash of a pedestrian being hit, along with a testimonial from someone affected by a red light crash (that was me). Sporting our logoed T-shirts, we set up an area with stickers, pens, and bookmarks with information about "Red Means Stop." I spoke about my ordeal of losing my mom to an audience of high school students. I was nervous to speak in front of such a large group, but happy to do so even if it meant only one person would think twice about running a red light. This is one of the last safe driving efforts I focused on. I had spent over two years pushing and now it was time to take a step back.

My focus had been shining a light on a negative in our society and how I believed it needed to change. Death, devastation of lives, and no accountability to drivers for causing it was heavy subject matter, especially when I was trying to grieve my own loss, but I was passionate about effecting change.

That said, I was tired of putting my energy to an unfavorable aspect and wanted to focus on a positive. I wanted to make an impact where I could see tangible results. I wanted to participate in something that wouldn't be met with contention. My youngest was struggling in school and my attention needed to shift to him. I felt guilty for giving up, for not trying as hard as I knew I could. When I set my mind to something and say it out loud, I am going to do it. Then I got the message that it was okay to change my mind. Sometimes what we set out to do changes direction and it is more about the journey than the end goal. I am more knowledgeable about the law-making process and safe driving efforts, and I met passionate advocates who made a difference in the world and, most of all, to me.

A few more safe driving efforts transpired after I hung up my hat. In 2011, the National Coalition for Safer Roads (NCSR) contacted me about making a video testimonial of the crash that killed my mom. NCSR works with traffic experts, engineers, law enforcement officials, and others to research and analyze red light, speed, and school bus stop arm safety cameras so that it can establish "best practices" for their use. They engage in awareness and education promotions that help inform the public of the benefits of safety cameras. The stories they were filming would demonstrate the impact of unsafe driving, attaching real faces of real victims to the research results. I was all for this. A camera crew filmed me at my house and at the crash site. I talked about my mom, the crash, and the impact of unsafe driving. As of 2020 the video is still posted on their website along with other testimonials.

While Riley was in high school, he took some video production classes and became adept at filming and editing. In 2013-2014 he created two public service announcement videos about distracted driving and the dangers of not paying attention behind the wheel. One video won an award at the high school film festival for best PSA and the other won an editing award in the Bridgestone Teen Safe Driving contest. He scored a brand new set of tires for his prize. For some this may not be much of an award, but to Riley he hit the jackpot. He collected wheels, like others collect shoes. He had several sets to change the look of his 1976 vintage BMW 2002. Tires were good winnings in his book. Safe driving messages were a family affair.

In 2015, The Red Means Stop Traffic Safety Alliance published a book about the dangers of red light running, statistics and stories of victims and survivors. My mom's story was included. The book is called *Carelessness Is No Accident? Consequences, Victims, No Closure.* I was happy to contribute to continue to raise awareness about the dangers of distracted driving and the impact we deal with when we lose a loved one from an avoidable crash where the driver has no consequences.

I will forever be altered by the choices of other people and their unsafe driving behavior. The impact transformed my life even before I was officially brought into this world. I recognize I have the choice in how I react, how I grieve, and how I heal. I wasn't ever sure I had the right recipe for restoration, but I do know if I listen to my gut, I can keep going another day.

CHAPTER 20:

Ever-changing Evolution

*"It's often the changes we didn't plan
for that change us the most."*
—UNKNOWN

Even though years have passed since I lost my mom, at times it's
like it was yesterday, and other times a lifetime ago. I have continued to brave pain, sorrow, grief, loss, and distress from other
happenings in my life. I am human, after all, and it's inevitable
that life's circumstances will be altered in some way. There were
times when change had been my choice and other times when
change had been brought upon me by no act of my own doing.

When I look around, I see change is fundamental in
our world. Spring is commencing and the trees are beginning
to effloresce, chartreuse green buds dotting their branches.
Crocus peek their purple coneheads out of the brown ground.
Robins are busy building nests to lay eggs and bring new life.

In a few hours, night will come, and I'll lay my head down to sleep. When the dawn of morning shines through my eastern windows I'll start my day again. Life is a conglomeration of events and patterns adding to the whole. There's harmony in this amalgamation.

I've weathered a multitude of loss and change since I healed from the death of my mom. Jon's dad and his Grandma Doris died, family members to me since I was sixteen years old. I went through the dissolution of my twenty-one-year marriage, which meant that the ideal I had for my family was over. I've had job loss, betrayals of trust, endings of relationships, witnessing my children struggle, emptiness (or empty nest) syndrome, loss of my youth as I approach fifty, and the passing of my pets Hector (Hector Molector), Pat (Patty Pooshka), Holly (Holly Klaveiner), and Etta (Etta May).

My dear Etta passed as I wrote the last couple chapters of this book. She was fourteen years old and the sweetest and most loving companion a dog owner could wish for. This is the first time in my life I can remember not having a fury friend by my side. With my empty nest, it was just the two of us rambling around the house together. I miss the clicking sound of her nails striking the hardwood floors, her snoring, and even her toots and hair clumps collecting as brown dust bunnies in the corners of rooms. It is eerily quiet without her and in the stillness, there is peace. Peace knowing she is no longer suffering in her ailing body.

My metamorphosis commenced when I suffered the intense loss of my mom. Her death unraveled all my patterns, disrupted my life, and revealed how much I had taken for granted. It affirmed what was most precious to me. A part of me died and then a rebirth occurred. My thoughts, perceptions, and how I chose to live my life with the time I had left changed. It opened me up to myself and how I truly wanted to live. A life with purpose and meaning. Focused on connections. Connections with people, nature, animals, myself and the mystery of it all. Where joy is a way of being.

I am passionate, inspired, and successful at developing and strengthening relationships with people who nurture my soul. Prosperity didn't come when I finally reached a goal or gained success, but rather in the journey along the way. The path of life involves other people who are collaborating, supporting, mentoring, and growing together. These are the people I find most energizing and enjoy spending my time with.

I have become more intentional about my thoughts, how I spend my time, and what I put my attention to. One of my only commodities is time and it is finite. We each have twenty-four hours in the day and the older I get I see how the days are numbered. When I evaluate a new job, relationship, the year ahead, trips, and even weekend outings, I like to write out my intentions. I focus on how I want to feel. Oftentimes in life I deduce things are going awry and anxiety may set in. Maybe I am working too much, not getting outside enough, or a relationship is out of sync. This is when I revisit what I wrote and how I wanted to feel at work, in my physical body, and in my relationships. I ponder why things are off and I develop a plan to get back on track. I may need to put more boundaries around work and what I say yes to, schedule time to be outside and take walks, make the time to be with friends. I find intentions, boundaries, and checking in on myself help me maintain the balance I desire.

I have found there is freedom in letting go. As humans we have a false sense of control. We get all twisted up wanting everything to go our way, for others to behave a certain way, and then to unravel why they didn't. There is an immense amount of energy wasted trying to control situations and others. It is an exhausting struggle and can cause anxiety, depression, and loss of relationships. If you can be open to the mystery of life and not judge, but rather receive what is happening, whatever it is, and bask in the freedom in letting go, then you will truly find security and courage. You will lead with trust instead of doubt and be open to what is.

The message from the medium Susan Driscoll after my mom passed was this: "It is time for you to slow down and stop being so busy and reflect on yourself. There's something to come out, the true you, the authentic you." I have reclaimed my authentic self. It has always been there and most likely got diverted by my ego and societal pressures I put upon myself. I look at children and see how playful, curious, carefree, and unbridled they are. This is home to me. I am continually seeking, questioning, researching, and learning. I love to be playful, goofy, and to laugh, especially at myself. I will forge ahead on this adventure and I look forward to discovering new possibilities for myself and the world, while procuring plenty of pleasure.

CHAPTER 21:

Leaving a Legacy

*"Legacy is not leaving something for people.
It's leaving something in people."*
—PETER STROPLE

When your parents die, you lose part of your childhood. Your identity is modified, and you are less of your parents and more of yourself. It can be a time for self-growth and transformation. You start to look at what you gained versus what was lacking in your relationship. You appreciate your parents more and your family's legacy. Unquestionably this happened to me. All the petty nitpicks that bothered me, or expectations I had about my mom, were released when she died. All of that was meaningless. What mattered was her essence and who she was in the world. For me she was a compassionate soul who made me feel loved, supported, seen, and heard. I like the quote I open this final chapter with, as it speaks to what's most important.

It isn't about the material possessions someone has left you. It is how they made you feel, touched your soul, and impacted your life. That's their legacy.

I was hoping to find some written words my mom had expressed through journals or letters she'd left behind, but there were none to be found. All I had were her to-do lists, handwritten recipes, and a few cards from her I had saved through the years. I wanted more from her. I wanted to know what moved her, what inspired her, what changed her, and what lessons she would want to share with me. It was that burning desire to continue to connect with her, to find my answers to these questions, that led me to start writing. After all, I did know how she expressed herself in the world. I knew how she wore her hair, painted her toes, tended her garden, decorated her home, and treated her family, friends, and animals. Her legacy lives on in me, in her grandsons, and in the other lives she touched. This book serves as a trace of her life and mine, a legacy in written form. I know she'd be proud of the results. My sons, too, will have something to better know her by, and to keep her legacy alive for their children.

I once read this list of regrets a hospice worker had collected while taking care of people at the end of their life. I find this list to be bittersweet:

- I wish I'd lived the life I had the courage to live. A life true to myself and not the life others expected of me.
- I wish I didn't work so hard.
- I wish I had the courage to express my feelings.
- I wish I'd stayed in touch with my friends.
- I wish I'd let myself be happier. Happiness is a choice.

Aloha is the Hawaiian salutation for hello and goodbye, but the literal definition has a deeper connotation. The word actually means "the presence of breath," or "the breath of life." It comes from "Alo," meaning presence, front, and face, and "ha," meaning breath. *Aloha* is a way of living and treating each other with love and respect. Its deep meaning starts by teaching ourselves to love our own beings first and afterwards to spread the love to others.

So it is with this sentiment I end this book, wishing each of you the best on your adventure of curiosity, self-discovery, connection, and love. Your heart will hold the truth and be your guide.

Aloha!